A JOURNEY INTO DIVINE LOVE

RABBI KIRT A. SCHNEIDER

CHARISMA HOUSE

For more resources like this, visit charismahouse.com and the author's website at DiscoveringtheJewishJesus.com.

Cataloging-in-Publication Data is on file with the Library of Congress.
International Standard Book Number: 978-1-63641-365-5
E-book ISBN: 978-1-63641-366-2

01 2024
Printed in the United States of America

Most Charisma Media products are available at special quantity discounts for bulk purchase for sales promotions, premiums, fund-raising, and educational needs. For details, call us at (407) 333-0600 or visit our website at www.charismamedia.com.

CONTENTS

PREFACE

MANY OF YOU are used to my expository, very literal type of teaching. The Song of Songs must be handled and taught in a different way because it is biblical poetry. And because it is poetry, it cannot be literally interpreted.

We need to acknowledge that the interpretation of the Song of Songs is not a precise science but rather a subjective, prophetic attempt to understand and apply it to our individual lives as we journey with Messiah into divine love. Please understand that my interpretation is not a "Thus saith the Lord" word, but I am confident you will find it helpful and beautiful and that it will be a blessing to your life. So please bear with me. Let's get started.

Chapter 1

A PROPHETIC LOVE LETTER

THE SONG OF Songs changed my life—and I believe it can change yours as well. I know that what I am about to share with you in the pages ahead may seem far-fetched, but I encourage you to open yourself up and come along with me on a beautiful journey into divine love.

For many years I couldn't get past what felt like significant barriers to my understanding and appreciation of the Song of Songs. My thoughts reflected that struggle: Does Jesus really want to know us the way a groom knows his bride? This feels uncomfortable to me, especially as a man. How can I see this theme as something healthy instead of something weird?

Does the rest of the Bible affirm this kind of intimate relationship with Jesus, or is this message isolated to the Song of Songs? In other words, how seriously should I take this perspective? And how do I apply a seemingly allegorical love poem between a man and a woman to my everyday walk with

Yeshua (Jesus)? What, if anything, does the Song have to do with my life today?

Before encountering the Song afresh, I certainly knew Yeshua as my Savior, Redeemer, Messiah, and friend. But I didn't understand the deeper mystery of His relationship with me as expressed in this book. Serious questions and reservations stood between me and the Song, and I'm sure this is why it has been one of the most neglected books in the Bible throughout history and in our own day.

Some Bible students and scholars even wonder why it is in the Bible! Aside from the fact that they don't find its flowery, poetic language appealing, they question whether King Solomon can teach us about pure marital love or even divine romance for that matter since he had hundreds of wives and concubines. For these reasons and many others, some sincere believers simply leave the book alone—or just read it through quickly in their Bible-in-a-year plans.

My view of the Song changed rather suddenly, however, when the Lord knitted my heart to this book in a way I never expected. In December some years back, I asked the Lord what I should focus on in His written Word in the coming new year. I was looking to Him for the next level of revelation He wanted to bring into my life. At that time I sensed the Lord beckoning me to give myself entirely to the study of the Song of Songs. I felt He was going to open up a new mystery to me. So I studied the book every day for fifty-two whole weeks.

Through the Song I have come to understand Jesus' love for me in a way I didn't truly see before. The Song of Songs opened up new vistas and shined a great deal of light on the kind of relationship God created for me—and you—to have with Him. I am confident the Holy Spirit will use the Song of Songs to unlock your own journey into divine love, providing personal breakthrough for you as He did for me.

The Song Through History

Where did the Song of Songs come from? How does it fit in with the rest of the Bible, and what are the limits and possibilities of its application in our own lives?

To begin with, some people are more familiar with the book being called the Song of Solomon or even the Book of Canticles. These are valid titles. I prefer Song of Songs because this book is—and forever will be—the greatest love song ever written on this side of eternity. It is the song of all songs, the pinnacle in form and message. In fact, the book's author actually names it the Song of Songs (Song 1:1), and it is called in Hebrew Shir Hashrim. (Throughout this book I will often refer to it simply as the Song.)

The rabbis have taught for centuries that among the wisdom books of the Hebrew Bible, Proverbs is like the outer court of the temple, Ecclesiastes is like the inner court, and the Song of Songs is like the holy of holies, meaning it reveals to us the deepest mysteries of divine love. The rabbis also teach that there are many different levels of understanding Scripture: the surface understanding, which is the purely natural reading, and other layers of revelation as you keep digging. This is certainly true when it comes to understanding the prophetic revelation of God's Word. Without forcing anything, we search for meanings under the surface.

Our Prophetic Destiny

On its face, the Song is simply a love letter or love poem Solomon wrote to the woman he was about to marry, called the Shulamite bride. This was one of more than a thousand songs he wrote as perhaps the most prolific songwriter of his age. The Song of Songs presents three main characters: Solomon, the Shulamite bride, and the daughters of Jerusalem. But of course we are not looking at it simply in the natural. We are interpreting it prophetically. I want to start by laying a foundation to help you receive the supernatural revelation of the Lord's love for you in this book. By looking at the Song prophetically rather than naturally, or merely as literature, your heart will be set ablaze in a new and profound way.

My belief, and the belief of many others, is that the Holy Spirit gave the Song of Songs to the church to help us understand Jesus' love for us. It uses the marriage relationship as a paradigm for the relationship we have entered into with Him both corporately and individually. The Song is a picture, then, of Christ and the church. How do we know this, and how can we say it with confidence? Let's look at 2 Peter 1:20–21, where the apostle Peter writes this:

> But know this first of all, that no prophecy of Scripture
> is a matter of one's own interpretation, for no prophecy
> was ever made by an act of human will, but men moved
> by the Holy Spirit spoke from God.

Peter affirmed that all Scripture is written by the Holy Spirit. The primary role of the Holy Spirit is to glorify Messiah Jesus and disclose the deep things of Yeshua to us. So it is inconceivable that the Holy Spirit would have given us a book in the Bible that was only about King Solomon's natural relationship with his wife. Rather, everything in Scripture speaks of Jesus. Men were "moved by the Holy Spirit," and they spoke and wrote about God.

Yeshua affirmed this in Luke 24, lending further confidence to our study of the Song as a prophetic book. At that moment in history, Jesus had been crucified and the disciples were downcast, not really understanding what had happened to Him. As best they could tell, Messiah Jesus was gone, and their plans had fallen to pieces. Then Luke relates this encounter:

> And behold, two of them were going that very day to a village named Emmaus, which was about seven miles from Jerusalem. And they were talking with each other about all these things which had taken place. While they were talking and discussing, Jesus Himself approached and began traveling with them. But their eyes were prevented from recognizing Him. And He said to them, "What are these words that you are exchanging with one another as you are walking?" And they stood still, looking sad.
>
> One of them, named Cleopas, answered and said to Him, "Are You the only one visiting Jerusalem and unaware of the things which have happened here in these days?" And He said to them, "What things?" And they said to Him, "The things about Jesus the Nazarene, who was a prophet mighty in deed and word in the sight of God and all the people, and how the chief priests and our rulers delivered Him to the sentence of death, and crucified Him. But we were hoping that it was He who

was going to redeem Israel. Indeed, besides all this, it is the third day since these things happened. But also some women among us amazed us. When they were at the tomb early in the morning, and did not find His body, they came, saying that they had also seen a vision of angels who said that He was alive. Some of those who were with us went to the tomb and found it just exactly as the women also had said; but Him they did not see."

And He said to them, "O foolish men and slow of heart to believe in all that the prophets have spoken! Was it not necessary for the Christ to suffer these things and to enter into His glory?" *Then beginning with Moses and with all the prophets, He explained to them the things concerning Himself in all the Scriptures.*

—LUKE 24:13–27, EMPHASIS ADDED

This tells us plainly that not only is all Scripture written by the Holy Spirit, but all Scripture is about Jesus! The entire Word of God finds its ultimate purpose in Yeshua. He is the center focus of the whole Bible. So the Song of Songs must be about Messiah Jesus or it would not be in the Bible. Yes, it is different from other types of books in Scripture. Some biblical books are meant primarily to convey history, some to lay a foundation for doctrine, some to impart wisdom, and still others to teach us how to have proper relationships with one another. But the Song of Songs reveals to us the heart and emotions of God more fully than any other book in the Bible.

Jesus foretells this in John's Gospel, saying that after He departs, He will send the Holy Spirit—the Ruach HaKodesh, who will then take the deep things of Yeshua's heart and reveal them to us.

Jesus put it this way:

> But when He, the Spirit of truth, comes, He will guide
> you into all the truth; for He will not speak on His own
> initiative, but whatever He hears, He will speak; and He
> will disclose to you what is to come. *He will glorify Me,*
> *for He will take of Mine and will disclose it to you.* All
> things that the Father has are Mine; therefore I said that
> He takes of Mine and will disclose it to you.
> —JOHN 16:13–15, EMPHASIS ADDED

So the Song of Songs is given to us by the Holy Spirit, its
main subject is Jesus, and we must interpret it with Him
foremost in mind. What, then, is the Song telling us about
Yeshua—and ourselves?

Heading for a Wedding

I do not believe Solomon knew when he wrote the Song of
Songs that he was bringing forth a revelation beyond the natural one he had in mind. We find many instances in Scripture
where people were moved by the Holy Spirit to speak and
write in an inspired way—and didn't even know it.

We see an example of this in John 11:47–51:

> Therefore the chief priests and the Pharisees convened a
> council, and were saying, "What are we doing? For this
> man is performing many signs. If we let Him go on like
> this, all men will believe in Him, and the Romans will
> come and take away both our place and our nation." But
> one of them, Caiaphas, who was high priest that year,
> said to them, "You know nothing at all, nor do you take
> into account that it is expedient for you that one man

die for the people, and that the whole nation not perish."
Now he did not say this on his own initiative, but being
high priest that year, he prophesied that Jesus was going
to die for the nation.

Caiaphas prophesied without knowing it. In a similar way,
I feel certain that when Solomon wrote the Song of Songs, he
was not aware he was prophesying by the Holy Spirit.

What exactly was the Holy Spirit prophesying through
Solomon, the wisest man who ever lived? On the surface the
Song depicts a romance taking place between a king and a
young maiden on a journey toward maturity. But in the context
of the rest of Scripture, and in alignment with the prophetic
nature of "all the Scriptures" (remember how Jesus opened the
Scriptures on the road to Emmaus, revealing Himself in every
book?), we can say that the Song of Songs speaks to the unpar-
alleled depth of relationship we as believers have with our
King, Jesus. We are His bride, journeying toward the marriage
supper of the Lamb (Rev. 19:9). Marital intimacy is the only
natural experience that approaches the close, loving relationship and partnership we were made to have with our Messiah.

What basis do we have for interpreting the Song of Songs as
depicting a marriage relationship between us and Jesus? For
a lot of believers the marriage paradigm is a foreign one. We
are accustomed to thinking in terms of salvation and going
to heaven, yet we have no real concept of spiritual intimacy
with Jesus. But the idea is central to Scripture. For example, in
Ephesians 5:28–32, Paul writes (emphasis added):

So husbands ought also to love their own wives as their
own bodies. He who loves his own wife loves himself;

for no one ever hated his own flesh, but nourishes and cherishes it, just as Christ also does the church, because we are members of His body. For this reason a man shall leave his father and mother and shall be joined to his wife, and the two shall become one flesh. *This mystery is great; but I am speaking with reference to Christ and the church.*

It would be one thing if Paul confined himself to teaching husbands how to treat their wives, but he took it to a whole other level. He unveiled a great mystery, which is that Christ and His church are exemplified in the earthly marriage relationship—the two become one. Our marriages are little, lived-out pictures of the kind of relationship Jesus intends to have with us! That is astonishing, and even Paul refers to it as a great mystery, something holy and profound.

God gets great delight from our union with Him. Consider this: Can you imagine Jesus marrying a bride from whom He receives no enjoyment? Who would be foolish enough to marry someone who does not move him! No, Messiah Jesus enjoys His bride just as Solomon enjoyed the Shulamite. Yeshua has emotions and is moved by our emotions. We see in Scripture that He greatly rejoiced in the Holy Spirit (Luke 10:21). At other times He wept (John 11:35). He was moved by the emotions of His people (Matt. 14:14). As in any close relationship, what we feel touches Him, and vice versa. This is perhaps the essence of a bridal relationship. The Song of Songs gives us the fullest revelation of the emotions of God. It helps us to understand how Jesus feels about us and how we also affect Him.

Beloved, we have feelings because God has feelings. We are created in His image. The fact that we crave love is because

God is love. Deep inside our hearts we crave romance and the experience of falling in love because God put that longing and need in each one of us. The reason He put it there is because He wants to fulfill it with Himself.

God has destined us to be married to Him, and this is what the Song of Songs is about. Every second of every day God is not just aware of us but keyed in on our emotions and thoughts. "The very hairs of your head are all numbered" (Luke 12:7). The journey into divine romance depicted in the Song of Songs is about our discovering that this relationship is real. We don't just get saved and go to heaven. We are the bride of Christ, His eternal partner, the joy of his heart.

Revelation 19:7–9 says: "'Let us rejoice and be glad and give the glory to Him, for the marriage of the Lamb has come and His bride has made herself ready.' It was given to her to clothe herself in fine linen, bright and clean; for the fine linen is the righteous acts of the saints. Then he said to me, 'Write, "Blessed are those who are invited to the marriage supper of the Lamb."' And he said to me, 'These are true words of God.'"

Considering that a climax of our salvation is the marriage supper of the Lamb, it only makes sense that the Holy Spirit would give us more revelation on this subject in the written Word of God. In 2 Corinthians 11:2, Paul writes, "For I am jealous for you with a godly jealousy; for I betrothed you to one husband, so that to Christ I might present you as a pure virgin." Paul was sensing the Lord's jealousy for us and used marriage language to explain it. Why is a husband jealous? Because he wants his wife all to himself. To have to share her with another would be betrayal and a breaking of intimacy. Paul felt this same type of jealousy for God's people, that they would be presented to Jesus undefiled and pure, having eyes only for Him.

Our salvation aims at one purpose: that you and I will experience such a deep relationship with Yeshua that we can only compare that type of love to the love between a husband and wife. We are on the journey into divine love. The Holy Spirit used Solomon to give the church an understanding of how God feels about us and the type of love relationship we are being called into. You and I are heading into a relationship with Jesus so deep and so close that we have not even begun to perceive the fullness of it. We were made and called to be the bride of the Messiah. The Song was given by the Holy Spirit, taken directly from the heart of Yeshua, to ignite within our hearts a deep understanding of and fiery passion for Jesus.

A Progressive Conversation

The Shulamite bride is a picture of you and me and of the body of Christ corporately. Together and individually, we are on a journey into divine love, and this journey is progressive, meaning it is unveiled and accomplished over time in different stages and steps. This revelation shows us how we, the bride, grow in our intimacy with Jesus, the Bridegroom. As a result of this progression, we eventually come to realize how we bring great pleasure and delight to Jesus.

In the beginning of the Song, the Shulamite bride—a type or shadow of the church—looks at Jesus mostly in terms of what He can do for her. Many of us start out in our walk with God thinking mostly about how it affects us. We want God to answer our prayers. We want Him to tell us about His plan for our lives. We want His blessing, His protection, His promotion, His presence—and all of that is good and necessary. But as the maiden grows in maturity, she sees it is not all about what God does for her but also about what the relationship means to Him.

She realizes that Yeshua gets enjoyment from His bride. What He wants more than anything else is our affections. They are a beautiful fragrance to Him.

As the bride grows in her spiritual maturity, she comes to understand that her affections touch His heart. Not only is she blessed when she feels His love, but He is blessed when He feels her love. It moves Him. He is sensitive to our love.

Like our relationship with Jesus, the Song of Songs reads dynamically. It is in fact a dialogue between lovers and reflects the conversational intimacy of husband and wife. In a living, real relationship, a husband speaks to his wife, and she responds to him; he answers back and so on. It is the same in the Song as they converse on the journey into divine love.

But the Song is more than a dialogue we read—it is a discourse we enter into to gain from personally. You and I must see ourselves in this story, and we must dialogue with the Holy Spirit about what we are learning and experiencing as we journey through. One good way is to get a notebook with plenty of space to write and bring it to this study with you. Whenever something occurs to you, set this book down and write your revelation—or question or prayer—in the notebook. It will become a precious testimony of your progress with Him into greater closeness.

For all these reasons—and many more that we shall see—I consider the Song to be one of the most important books in the entire Word of God. I believe God is emphasizing this revelation now to His church because we are approaching the end of the age. To walk steadfast and remain in His love during the days ahead, we must have the revelation that the Father gives us in the Song of Songs deeply imparted into us: the revelation of how our Maker feels about us—that He is in love with us and has called and destined the church to be His bride.

Before we dive in, I invite you to begin with a prayer:

> *Father God, I ask that You will open my heart as I journey in Your Word through the Song of Songs. Anoint me to receive the revelation of Your beauty and love for me as I study and take in this teaching. Open my heart, and change me with a revelation of Your fiery love.*
>
> *I ask You to strengthen my heart in Your love as I receive Your Word through the Song of Songs. I am not looking for information. I am not content just to have knowledge. I want revelation to touch my heart and sink deep down into my inner man. Transform me by Your love. Abba, bring me into divine love! I will run after You!*

Chapter 2

KISS ME WITH YOUR REVELATION

Hardly anything is better than those first feelings of falling in love. A new—and perhaps unexpected—interest kindles in our hearts. Our emotions and desires are stirred, amazing and even frightening us sometimes. Flutters of excitement cause us to say and do things we wouldn't under "normal" circumstances. Suddenly, we find ourselves on a pathway of new discovery, and so the journey of love begins.

Many people, Christians included, don't realize that Jesus Himself is on a journey of love with each one of us. His deep, personal interest in His beloved ones is never casual or offhand. He has committed Himself to having the closest fellowship imaginable with us individually and corporately. While we may be inclined to keep Jesus at arm's length, He is content with nothing less than communing with us in the deepest ways possible. The good news is that He is totally committed to helping us love Him as fully as He loves us. This is the purpose of the Christian life—and the Song of Songs.

Who Is in This Song?

To briefly recap, three main characters speak in the Song. The king, who in the natural was King Solomon, is a prophetic shadow of the Bridegroom King, Jesus. The second character is the bride he will marry, called the Shulamite bride in the Song. This is where things get really exciting because the Shulamite woman is not some fictional character—she was a real woman, and prophetically she is you and me! She represents every believer and the church as a whole. Beloved, the Song of Songs is literally God's love letter to you and everyone who has come to faith through Jesus Christ. The Song of Songs is personal for each of us, as if we were the only ones in existence.

This may be a stretch for some. You may have a hard time buying that the Song of Songs speaks to you personally or that God expresses His love for us through a marital paradigm. But I want to stress again that this book must not just impart information or even revelation to you but rather spur an ongoing dialogue between you and King Jesus. If all you get from this book is knowledge, then I have failed. Rather, we must turn these verses and their revelation into a prayer dialogue.

Like the Shulamite bride, who keeps calling out to her beloved (King Solomon) and waiting for his response, we will pause at times to call out to the Holy Spirit, then listen for His voice to answer. The Song of Songs cannot be profitably studied from afar. It draws us close and invites us into the original heart relationship for which God created us. We must inhabit it and let it become the words of our hearts toward Jesus.

The third character—or really, characters—in the Song are the daughters of Jerusalem, representing believers who are less mature. We will look at each of these characters in more depth as we go along.

Awakening Desire

The Song begins with the bride telling us right away that she desires the kisses of her Beloved, as she declares boldly, "May he kiss me with the kisses of his mouth!" (Song 1:2). Let's look at the opening verses of this Song:

> The Song of Songs, which is Solomon's. "May he kiss me with the kisses of his mouth! For your love is better than wine. Your oils have a pleasing fragrance, your name is like purified oil; therefore the maidens love you."
>
> —SONG 1:1–3

The first thing that happens to each of us on the journey of love is that we experience a new desire for intimacy. What sufficed yesterday no longer satisfies today. We crave something else, something more. Our hearts are awakened to new possibilities of nearness. Like the Shulamite bride, we call out, "Kiss me! I want to be closer to You than ever before."

So the Song starts out beautifully with the Shulamite bride—who, again, is a prophetic shadow of the church—calling out for the Bridegroom's kisses.

To some readers, this seems unduly personal, especially for a book of the Bible. Why would the bride be so candid about her awakening desire? What does she know that we don't? Why is she so passionate about Messiah Jesus? Where does this hunger come from? The answer is, she had encountered Yeshua and discovered that He is good.

So she cried out to go deeper into the love of her Bridegroom King. When people say things like "Religion is boring," "Following Jesus seems uninteresting," or "Reading the Bible doesn't do anything for me," I know they have never truly encountered Him. He has never made Himself real to that person in some way, because once Jesus makes Himself real to you, it will elicit in you a passion to encounter Him again and in new ways.

I remember being a young Jewish person back in 1978. I knew nothing about Yeshua, but one night when I was twenty years old the Lord appeared to me in a vision. It happened in the middle of a summer night. No one had witnessed to me. I had never read the New Testament. Jesus wasn't even on my radar screen. I was a Jew. I never thought about Jesus. But Yeshua revealed Himself to me. I relate this life-changing experience in my book *Called to Breakthrough*. The point is that when I had that vision of Jesus, I knew the Lord was real, and I wanted more. I didn't understand Christian doctrine yet. I had never read the Bible—but I hungered for more of what I had experienced, or rather who I had experienced.

All love for Jesus begins when Yeshua inspires that love. The Bible says we didn't love Him first, but rather we love Him because He first loved us and shed His love abroad in our hearts (1 John 4:19; Rom. 5:5). These encounters with His love don't have to happen in visions or in the middle of the night. Messiah Jesus encounters people in many different ways. Sometimes He does it when we are reading the Bible and we feel the Holy Spirit touching our hearts. He may speak to us through the words of a friend. He may come to us in some type of mystical way, in a dream, or in a deeply personal experience of His presence. But however it happens, once you know He is real, you will want more.

That is what happened to the Shulamite bride. She had experienced the King in her "chamber," which she mentions a few verses later. That initial encounter rendered her love-sick, longing for more interaction with Him. Even as I write this, I am asking God to release into your heart a supernatural knowledge through divine revelation, that you would know Messiah Jesus loves you, He is real, He is alive, and you can experience greater measures of Him here and now, not just in heaven in the sweet by-and-by. Like the Shulamite bride, we can proclaim that the King has brought us into His chamber and left us longing for a closer relationship with Him!

Let me stop and ask you, Is anything in the way of you having greater closeness with Jesus? For some it may be a boyfriend or girlfriend. You know the relationship is bad for you, and you know it makes you miserable, but you're almost addicted to it. For others a job or career may be interfering with a deeper pursuit of God. For some it's alcohol, drug abuse, cigarettes, vaping, lying, cheating, internet pornography, gambling, or whatever sin is distracting and hurting you. It is time to let those things go! When you get a taste of the reality of Jesus, you realize nothing truly compares.

The Ways He Kisses Us

Notice that the bride's desire was for "the kisses of his mouth." There are various types of kisses in Scripture. For example, we read in the Book of Romans that we are to greet one another with a holy kiss, which is the kiss of a friend. There's also a kiss of affection and care between a parent and his or her children. In some cultures people greet each other with kisses on the cheek when they meet. But then there are the kisses of the mouth; this refers to the intimate kiss. This is the kiss of love.

Right up front I want to ask you to reject every sensual interpretation of the Song. This book has nothing to do with physical sexuality with God. Rather, it uses human experience to prophesy and describe what Paul called a great mystery, that is, the love of Jesus for His bride, the church. His interest in us is not sexual but spiritual.

With that in mind, what do these intimate kisses represent? They speak of the words that proceed from Jesus' mouth. Remember that the Lord told the children of Israel, "Man does not live by bread alone, but man lives by everything that proceeds out of the mouth of the LORD" (Deut. 8:3). Rabbis call these words the "kisses of the Torah," which are the revelation of God and His love to our hearts. This is what we are talking about—Messiah Jesus touching my heart and yours by His Word with the revelation of His love.

These words are living and active, Hebrews 4:12 tells us. When the Holy Spirit touches our hearts, it is the Word that touches us. Jesus is the embodiment of the Word, as John wrote in the first two verses of his Gospel: "In the beginning was the Word [Jesus], and the Word was with God, and the Word was

God. He was in the beginning with God." The Word became flesh. So we are asking not for physical kisses or simple thrills but the kiss of the enduring revelation of Jesus' love for us.

This speaks of communion at every level possible. The Word of God is the expression of the thoughts of God. It is the manifestation of God Himself. Behind every word is a thought, because you can't have a meaningful word without a thought behind it. When the Shulamite bride calls out to be kissed with the kisses of His mouth, she is actually saying, "Reveal Your heart to me. Reveal Your thoughts to me. Reveal how You feel about me, Lord Jesus." This must be our cry: "O, kiss me, Yeshua, with the kisses of Your mouth. I want to encounter You. Make Yourself real to me. Touch my heart so I know You're alive. Touch my heart so I can feel Your love for me. Make Yourself known and felt."

Let's pause for a moment and pray that He will do this work in our lives:

> *Messiah Jesus, I thank You that You are revealing Your love to me even now, and I ask You to continue in an ever-greater way to unveil to my heart the mystery of Your love for me, that You would in an ever-increasing way kiss me with the kisses of Your mouth.*

Yeshua already promised to respond to this prayer. In John 17:26, He said to the Father, "I have made Your name known to them, and will make it known." In this verse, He promises to continue revealing the heart of God to all mankind! Why does He do it? He tells us in the same verse: "so that the love with which You loved Me may be in them, and I in them."

Isn't that amazing? It's as if Yeshua was responding to the cry of the Shulamite bride written in this Song nearly a thousand years before His earthly birth. I believe Solomon was prophesying God's desire for relationship with His people, and when Jesus came He manifested Father's nature and name to us so that the love with which the Father loved Yeshua may be in us.

Better Than All Other Pleasures

The Shulamite bride then declares in chapter 1, verse 2 of the Song, "For your love is better than wine." With this declaration we know the Shulamite bride has tried the pleasures of the world and found them lacking compared to the sweetness of her Beloved. Wine is the symbol and shadow of earthly pleasures. It can mean sinful pleasures, because the Bible says sin is pleasurable for a season. It feels good to sin, but the end result is death—everyone who sins pays the piper for their "pleasure." This world gives only cheap, temporary thrills. They are tiresome and never live up to their promise. You always feel cheated by their deceitful enjoyments.

But the wine she refers to also means the legitimate pleasures God gives us to enjoy. Yeshua's first miracle was to turn water into wine. The Bible often refers to wine as a way of speaking about the blessings the Lord gives us circumstantially. These are good things. But they also pale in comparison with the experience of God's presence and the love of Jesus. All the blessings and favor God gives you in this life—in your relationships, health, finances, hobbies, and so on—are important and honorable, but even these cannot compare to the blessing of relationship with God Himself.

This is what the apostle Paul wrote about in Philippians 3:7–11:

But whatever things were gain to me, those things I have counted as loss for the sake of Christ. More than that, I count all things to be loss in view of the surpassing value of knowing Christ Jesus my Lord, for whom I have suffered the loss of all things, and count them but rubbish so that I may gain Christ, and may be found in Him, not having a righteousness of my own derived from the Law, but that which is through faith in Christ, the righteousness which comes from God on the basis of faith, that I may know Him and the power of His resurrection and the fellowship of His sufferings, being conformed to His death; in order that I may attain to the resurrection from the dead.

Paul had experienced great success and renown within his community as a young man. He said he had been "circumcised the eighth day, of the nation of Israel, of the tribe of Benjamin, a Hebrew of Hebrews; as to the Law, a Pharisee; as to zeal, a persecutor of the church; as to the righteousness which is in the Law, found blameless" (Phil. 3:5–6). He said he was "educated under Gamaliel, strictly according to the law of [his] fathers, being zealous for God" (Acts 22:3) and "was advancing in Judaism beyond many of [his] contemporaries among [his] countrymen, being more extremely zealous for [his] ancestral traditions" (Gal. 1:14).

Then the unexpected took place: Messiah Jesus came to Paul on the road to Damascus. Paul wasn't searching for Yeshua. In fact, he was an avowed enemy of this new sect and was traveling around finding Jewish Christians to imprison. But that day a blinding light came and knocked Paul off his horse, and Jesus spoke to Paul and said, "Shaul, Shaul"—for that was his

Hebrew name at the time—"get up and enter the city, and it will be told you what you must do" (Acts 9:6).

All the good things Paul had achieved and received in life didn't hold a candle to the life and love he now experienced in relationship with Jesus. His heart was ravished. He could pursue nothing else. So, he wrote later, he counted all those prior blessings and honors as loss; they were nothing in light of the surpassing value of knowing Messiah Jesus. He lost his family, his friends, and his standing in the religious community, yet he counted them as rubbish compared to the superior knowledge of Yeshua and His love.

That is exactly what happened with the bride in the Song of Songs. She had a revelation of divine love. She was touched by the kisses of God. She was able to apprehend what Paul prayed in Ephesians 3:18–19, that we would all be able to comprehend "the breadth and length and height and depth, and to know the love of Christ which surpasses knowledge, that [we] may be filled up to all the fullness of God."

She recognized that Yeshua's love is better than anything else in life. This is the love to which the Song of Songs calls the church and each one of us. Once we get a taste of Messiah Jesus, we are ruined for any inferior blessing or pleasure. Like the bride, we are so undone by Him that we can't concentrate or focus on anything else but pursuing Him, and we cry out as she did: "Kiss me with the kisses of Your mouth! For Your love is better than wine."

Those things that used to occupy or enslave us drop away as we run after Jesus. His love gives us the capacity to let those things go. Earthly pursuits, relationships, success—they all fade into the background of our lives. Food, hobbies, and entertainment now seem second-rate compared to the satisfaction we experience in relating to our Beloved. There simply is no substitute for being touched by God with the kisses of His mouth.

The Fragrance of the Beloved

This total satisfaction spurred the bride to praise the Bridegroom openly:

> Your oils have a pleasing fragrance, your name is like purified oil; therefore the maidens love you.
>
> —SONG 1:3

Once we experience Yeshua, who Himself is love, we can't help but speak of His excellencies. We do our best to describe the essence of who He is, as the Shulamite bride did. Consider what a fragrance is, whether of a flower or oil or anything else. A fragrance is actually the essence of the thing itself. It expresses its internal makeup to our nostrils. When we smell the fragrance of a flower, we are smelling what the flower is. So the bride here is saying, "Jesus, You are so beautiful inside. Your fragrance is so lovely. The essence of who You are is pleasing and pure, eliciting love in all who encounter You."

Shortly after first encountering Messiah Yeshua, I ran into a woman who sprinkled the words of Jesus into her conversation. She wasn't a Christian but a follower of New Age beliefs. She wasn't referring to Jesus in the biblical sense of who He is, but every now and then she would mention His name as if He were merely a prophet or wise man. But whenever she said "Jesus," it was as if the Holy Spirit filled the name with beautiful music. She would be talking along and all her words would be lifeless, and as soon as she said the name Jesus, it jumped out from the rest of the sentence, was lifted up, and filled with beautiful, heavenly music. At least that's how my awakened heart perceived it.

That is what the bride does here. She praises the beautiful name of Jesus, speaking it forth like a fragrance, exalting its purity and essence. When you do that, people are drawn to the Spirit's essence, much as they are drawn to the beautiful fragrance of flowers. We fall deeper in love with Yeshua as we encounter His presence.

Cry Out

As we close this chapter, I encourage you to do as the Shulamite bride did and call out to Yeshua in response to the revelation you have so far received through the Song. May your cry be:

> *Lord, bring me close and give me even greater revelation of Your love for me! Show me Your nature and personality. Let me praise You for who You are so others may come to experience You for themselves.*
>
> *Lord Jesus, ignite a passion and hunger within me where currently I have none, or have too little. Give me a chamber experience with You as the Shulamite bride had so that I may cry out as she did, "Kiss me with the kisses of Your mouth!" I want to encounter Your Word like never before. Come and disclose Yourself to me.*
>
> *Yeshua, I am asking You to make Yourself known to me in a very real way. I want to feel and*

experience You. I want to declare that I know no greater pleasure on earth than the pleasure of communing with and learning from You. I want to see in greater measure the purity of Your character and love.

Father God, Your Word says that Your invisible attributes—Your fragrances—are clearly seen in the world You have created. When I look at the world, I see Your great beauty expressed in every natural way through Your creation. This beauty is Your fragrance.

Give me now greater revelation of how beautiful You are. Let me experience Your beautiful essence that my heart would unfold to You more. Make known to me through the kisses of Your mouth— through the Word who has become flesh, the Lord Jesus—the fullness of the revelation of Your love for me. Help me to understand how You feel about me and all Your children. Messiah Jesus, kiss me, I pray, with the kisses of Your mouth. Make my heart fully alive to You. Awaken me to Your love. Thank You! Amen and amen.

Chapter 3

DRAW ME AFTER YOU

A S THE SHULAMITE bride encounters the King and falls in love with Him, she says, "Draw me after you and let us run together!" (Song 1:4).

What is happening here? She is setting the course of her life and declares that she has two life goals. First, she wants Yeshua to continue to draw her to Himself. She gives Him permission to pry her hands loose from anything she is hanging on to that keeps her apart from Him. She wants Him to brush aside every hindrance that stands between them. This is a prayer all of us should pray regularly. Jesus said in John 6 that no one comes to Him unless the Father draws him. It is a biblical truth that we can't come to Yeshua unless the Holy Spirit, the Ruach HaKodesh, draws us to Him.

The Shulamite bride wisely says, "God, I don't have the power to come to You on my own. There are things in the way that keep me from fully giving myself to You, things I am hanging on to, things I am afraid to let go of, even things I am addicted to. But You are stronger than my weaknesses. Draw me after You so nothing separates me from Your love." May this be our constant prayer as He draws us ever closer.

Her second life goal is to participate with Him in building the kingdom, so she asks that they would "run together." She wants to partner with Him for His purposes on the earth. She wants His assignment to become her assignment. Messiah Jesus spoke of this reality in John 17:3–4 when He said, "This is eternal life, that they may know You, the only true God, and Jesus Christ whom You have sent. I glorified You on the earth, having accomplished the work which You have given Me to do."

Being a disciple of Jesus involves sharing in His ministry on earth. Just as Yeshua came to earth to fulfill the Father's assignment, so our assignment on earth is to continue the work of Christ. Jesus said to His disciples, "As the Father has sent Me, I also send you" (John 20:21).

Knowing God and doing His work are inextricably tied together. We are His light on earth right now. We are the body of Messiah in this age! We co-labor with Jesus on this earth, winning the lost; offering deliverance; serving as instruments of love, healing, and peace; and standing as bastions of the Holy Spirit's presence. Jesus said: "Truly, truly, I say to you, he who believes in Me, the works that I do, he will do also; and greater works than these he will do; because I go to the Father" (John 14:12). So the bride's other life goal is to do the works— and greater works—of God in close partnership with Him.

In the same way, our lives and journeys into divine love involve a balance of spending time alone with God ("draw me") and doing His work ("run together"). "Draw me" looks like sitting with Him every day, listening to beautiful worship music, being silent before Him, reading His Word, listening to messages preached, and spending time in fellowship with other followers of Yeshua.

"Let us run together" is doing the works of the gospel He has prepared in advance for us to do, serving in all manner of ways beginning with our own family and friends. We will talk throughout this book about finding the balance between "draw me" and "let us run together," but for now we must start to align our vision with the Shulamite bride's vision, expressed in Song of Songs 1:4, which we can paraphrase this way: "Draw me after You, Lord Jesus. I want to know You, to be one with You in love, and to run with You in this world and complete the work You have assigned me to do."

Drawn Into His Chambers

Messiah Yeshua responds to the maiden's requests by drawing her into His chambers, with the Son again using bridal language to describe their relationship.

> The king has brought me into his chambers.
>
> —Song 1:4

This is a beautiful example of the fulfillment of Jesus' words:

> Ask, and it will be given to you; seek, and you will find; knock, and it will be opened to you. For everyone who asks receives, and he who seeks finds, and to him who knocks it will be opened. Or what man is there among you who, when his son asks for a loaf, will give him a

31

stone? Or if he asks for a fish, he will not give him a snake, will he? If you then, being evil, know how to give good gifts to your children, how much more will your Father who is in heaven give what is good to those who ask Him!

—MATTHEW 7:7–11

James the apostle said, "Draw near to God and He will draw near to you" (Jas. 4:8). And Yeshua said, "He who has My commandments and keeps them is the one who loves Me; and he who loves Me will be loved by My Father, and I will love him and will disclose Myself to him.…If anyone loves Me, he will keep My word; and My Father will love him, and We will come to him and make Our abode with him. He who does not love Me does not keep My words; and the word which you hear is not Mine, but the Father's who sent Me" (John 14:21, 23–24).

All of these are ways of describing the same chamber experience the Shulamite bride is invited to partake of in the Song. As your heart increases in anticipation and expectation of being with Jesus and working with Him, you will have more of these "bridal chamber" experiences, where Messiah Jesus lets you feel His love. The Holy Spirit will bear witness with your spirit of His nearness, His beauty, and how much He loves you. There is nothing like it in all the earth!

Aren't you thankful that God reveals Himself to us during our lives on this earth? It is true that now we see through a glass dimly, but that doesn't mean we have to wait for heaven to experience God's glory. No, Ephesians 1:14 says we've been given the Holy Spirit as a pledge of our inheritance. The Holy

Spirit gives us foretastes of the things conferred to us by God. As it is written:

> But we speak God's wisdom in a mystery, the hidden wisdom which God predestined before the ages to our glory; the wisdom which none of the rulers of this age has understood; for if they had understood it they would not have crucified the Lord of glory; but just as it is written, "Things which eye has not seen and ear has not heard, and which have not entered the heart of man, all that GOD has prepared for those who love Him."
>
> For to us God revealed them through the Spirit; for the Spirit searches all things, even the depths of God. For who among men knows the thoughts of a man except the spirit of the man which is in him? Even so the thoughts of God no one knows except the Spirit of God. Now we have received, not the spirit of the world, but the Spirit who is from God, so that we may know the things freely given to us by God, which things we also speak, not in words taught by human wisdom, but in those taught by the Spirit, combining spiritual thoughts with spiritual words.
>
> —1 CORINTHIANS 2:7–13

Think about it, beloved ones: we can know the things freely given to us by God, by the Spirit of God. What a blessing!

I encourage you to go a step further and ask Yeshua to give you intimate Bridegroom chamber experiences. Perhaps you feel that you've never had one. Or maybe you have had encounters with Jesus, but it has been a long time. Or perhaps you have had wonderful experiences even recently. Maybe the Lord revealed Himself to you in a dream, while you were talking with another person, in a worship service, or while you were out in nature. Messiah Jesus can make Himself known in any number of ways.

Let's turn this desire into a spoken prayer right now.

> *King Jesus, reveal Yourself to me in chamber experiences. I praise You today and thank You for everything You've already done—for wooing and drawing me. I thank You for bringing me to this place, and now I'm asking You, my Bridegroom, to reveal more of Yourself to me. Even as the Shulamite bride said the King brought her into His chambers, I am asking You by Your Spirit to give me chamber experiences, to give me fresh manna. Make Yourself known; make Yourself felt as I repent of all sluggishness and slothfulness in seeking You. Help me to encounter You in a brand-new or renewed way.*

Deciding to Be Glad

After she is brought into the bridal chamber, the Shulamite declares, "We will rejoice in you and be glad" (Song 1:4). If you and I want to be in close fellowship with God, we must make a commitment to be glad in His love. We need to declare as she did, "You are a good God, and I am committing now to be glad in my life."

You see, being glad is a decision. In today's superficial world people are moved by every circumstance. We set our affections on things that shift and fail us. It is a great tragedy that sometimes the more we have, the shallower our lives seem to become and the shakier our emotional frameworks.

Years ago in the 1980s, I had a vision of the night while staying at a friend's house in West Virginia. The vision lasted all of one second, but it was so powerful I never forgot it. While I was sleeping, I saw a glorious warship on the ocean at night. I observed it from above as if I were looking over the front of the craft. It was beautiful and majestic, a battleship cutting steadily through the ocean in the darkness. The vision was so graphic, and I knew from the Holy Spirit that the ship represented me. He was saying, "You are that warship, cutting through the ocean at night. You live in a dark world, but you are a warrior, and you have victory over this world even as that warship has victory on that dark ocean at night."

I am happy to say that the vision is for every true believer! Our surroundings can be dark and cold, as they were for that warship. But we choose the weapon of joy in the midst of imperfect circumstances. We live in a fallen world, in a dark age in which we have the privilege of declaring that "we will rejoice and be glad." This is the exact language used at the marriage supper of the Lamb in Revelation 19:6–7 when it is said, "Hallelujah! For the Lord our God, the Almighty, reigns. Let us rejoice and be glad and give the glory to Him, for the marriage of the Lamb has come and His bride has made herself ready."

We are happy warriors! Too many people have lost sight of the truth that we can live empowered over circumstances, that things don't always have to go right for us to be glad. Circumstances don't have to line up for us to have peace. There is a greater resource that can give us victory above every circumstance, and that is the power and presence of Jesus we receive in chamber encounters. Like the bride in the Song, we emerge from these moments saying, "We *will* rejoice in You and be glad."

I love the word *will* there because it reminds us that being joyful is a choice. You may say, "Is it possible for us to choose to be glad? How does that work?" People do it all the time. At work, when two people are arguing and the boss walks in, like a switch being thrown they change their attitudes, put on smiles, and act like nothing is wrong. That's how it's done. Yes, the choice may feel forced at first, but faking it in this case really does lead to making it real! We all have a will and are commanded to choose our attitudes and emotions. We are told to be thankful and glad and to rejoice always. Like the precious maiden in the Song, we must choose to be glad.

There is a man I've known for many years who has had very little money in his life and has dealt with many difficult issues. Yet every time I have seen him over the years—in the midst of cars breaking down, financial problems, health issues, and so on—he always says something to me like, "Praise God! It's another great day to be alive on the planet. Blessed be the name of the King." His face radiates with this simple truth that we are called to be glad just as God is glad. This man had made up his mind to do just that. You and I can do the same.

Remember His Love

The Shulamite bride then says, "We will remember thy love" (Song 1:4, KJV). This is a good time to pull out your journal, because the maiden here is demonstrating the importance of remembering.

Think about it. She had been brought into the bridal chamber. She had experienced the King in a wonderful, deeply personal way. Her heart unfolded to Him. She felt His arms around her, and at that point she declared, "I will remember Your love." She was saying, "I won't forget! I will go out of my way to make a record and keep a memory of the perfect ways in which You have met me and worked on my behalf."

We see people make this type of commitment throughout the Hebrew Bible. When the Lord did something special for the children of Israel, they would build a memorial for Him. They put a rock or a pile of rocks in a certain place as an altar—a permanent testimony to what God had done. They remembered what He did and talked about it every time they saw the altar. One of the most beautiful examples of this is in the Book of Joshua, after the Israelites crossed the Jordan River.

> Now when all the nation had finished crossing the Jordan, the LORD spoke to Joshua, saying, "Take for yourselves twelve men from the people, one man from each tribe, and command them, saying, 'Take up for yourselves twelve stones from here out of the middle of the Jordan, from the place where the priests' feet are standing firm, and carry them over with you and lay them down in the lodging place where you will lodge tonight.'"
>
> So Joshua called the twelve men whom he had appointed from the sons of Israel, one man from each tribe; and Joshua said to them, "Cross again to the ark of the LORD your God into the middle of the Jordan, and each of you take up a stone on his shoulder, according to the number of the tribes of the sons of Israel. Let this be a sign among you, so that when your children ask later, saying, 'What do these stones mean to you?' then you

shall say to them, 'Because the waters of the Jordan were cut off before the ark of the covenant of the LORD; when it crossed the Jordan, the waters of the Jordan were cut off.' So these stones shall become a memorial to the sons of Israel forever."

Thus the sons of Israel did as Joshua commanded, and took up twelve stones from the middle of the Jordan, just as the LORD spoke to Joshua, according to the number of the tribes of the sons of Israel; and they carried them over with them to the lodging place and put them down there. Then Joshua set up twelve stones in the middle of the Jordan at the place where the feet of the priests who carried the ark of the covenant were standing, and they are there to this day.

—JOSHUA 4:1–9

Beloved ones, do not lose track of what God has done for you! Journal it, make an audio or video record of it, email someone about it, post it on social media, make a plaque, post a note on your fridge, stick a note in your Bible—whatever you do, treasure those encounters and revelations God gives you. Not only does it delight and honor God, but it strengthens you in the future.

Yeshua warned that the enemy will come and try to steal the memory of your encounter. In the Book of Matthew, He told a parable about a sower who cast seed on different types of ground. One type of soil didn't preserve and protect the seed because it was too hard, and immediately the devil came and stole it. (See Matthew 13.) This is the testimony of far too many people. They hear the gospel and may even feel a touch from God and shed a tear, but they do not remember it with enough care and vigilance to keep it from being stolen out of their hearts. They go back to the way they were, with only a faint memory of that shining moment when the good news encountered their hearts.

When God touches you in some way, one of two things will happen when the enemy tries to steal it: either you will give up the memory and become weaker than you were before, or your tenacity in holding on to the impact of that event will make you stronger than you were before. This happened when Jesus was baptized in water by John the Baptist and had that wonderful encounter with the Holy Spirit and the Father. The enemy brazenly and immediately tried to steal it from Him. Jesus resisted the devil in the wilderness for forty days and forty nights, and then came out of the wilderness "in the power of the Spirit" (Luke 4:14). Because He held firmly to what the Father had done and said in that precious encounter in the Jordan River, He emerged from the time of trial stronger than before.

The bridal chamber becomes our place of promotion, where God builds new strength in us so we can withstand testing. Our weapon is remembering. When He was tempted in the wilderness, Yeshua remembered the Scriptures and spoke them to the devil to gain victory. We do the same when we do as the Shulamite maiden did and remember His love. We remember when He touched us. We remember prophetic words given to us and dreams from the Holy Spirit. We remember what the Lord has spoken to us in the past.

Remembering is not something God will do for us. We are to be involved in the process. Paul commanded us, "Work out your salvation with fear and trembling" (Phil. 2:12). We do not accomplish our own salvation, but we must participate in it and choose to remember what Yeshua has done for us when we face the onslaught of darkness. We are like that warship in my dream, journeying through the night. We war by thanking God for everything He's done in the past. We treasure and remember those chamber times.

Beloved, we need to write down and remember the things God has done in our lives. Then we will be strengthened to say, "I will be glad," and we will be empowered to choose to be victorious in our Messiah King.

I encourage you to turn this revelation into a dialogue with Yeshua.

> *Lord Jesus, I thank You that You draw Your church to Yourself. I thank You for drawing us, corporately and individually, even now. I declare that I will be glad and I will remember! I will not let the enemy steal the joy or the memory of what You have done for me.*
>
> *Right now, let me reflect on and honor the ways You have brought me through to victory. Give me unwavering confidence that You will do it again, and may Your joy remain my strength!*

Chapter 4

DARK YET LOVELY

THE SHULAMITE MAIDEN has been touched by the love of the King and is maturing in the initial steps on the journey into this divine romance. Now she has a twofold revelation about herself:

> I am dark, but lovely, O daughters of Jerusalem, like the tents of Kedar, like the curtains of Solomon. Do not look upon me, because I am dark, because the sun has tanned me.
>
> —Song 1:5–6, NKJV

What does all this mean? Let's work through the layers. In a natural sense, she was saying she was dark from working in the fields all day. Because she didn't have much money and occupied a lower rung on the economic ladder, she had to work outdoors and so had been tanned by the sun. She could not hide this fact, and it made her feel self-conscious and unattractive. Her words let us know that she was seeing things about herself that made her ashamed.

Yet on a deeper level, the insecurity she felt because of the darkness of her skin speaks of the fact that we all have sin in our lives. Jesus told those seeking to stone a woman caught in adultery, "He who is without sin among you, let him be the first to throw a stone at her" (John 8:7). One by one her accusers walked away. We all have sin in our lives. As believers we have declared war on sin; we do not willingly tolerate it, but we must continually battle against it. With the words "I am dark," the Shulamite is prophetically speaking to her realization that there are still issues in her life that need to be cleansed. She is not perfect yet, and walking with Yeshua has shone a light on those areas, which initially makes her uncomfortable.

The maiden felt the same tension you and I experience. Jeremiah the prophet wrote, "The heart is more deceitful than all else and is desperately sick; who can understand it?" (Jer. 17:9). There is darkness within the human heart. Paul told us that within him was an impulse that pushed him to do good and another that prompted him to do evil:

> For I know that nothing good dwells in me, that is, in my flesh; for the willing is present in me, but the doing of the good is not. For the good that I want, I do not do, but I practice the very evil that I do not want. But if I am doing the very thing I do not want, I am no longer the one doing it, but sin which dwells in me....Wretched man that I am! Who will set me free from the body of this death? Thanks be to God through Jesus Christ our Lord!
>
> —Romans 7:18–20, 24–25

Paul elsewhere called himself the chief of sinners! (See 1 Timothy 1:15.) The more we walk in the light of Yeshua and the closer we are to Him, the more the Holy Spirit will reveal to us the darkness in our hearts. For many new believers this starts with a conviction that they should quit drinking or smoking or living an immoral lifestyle. As we progress in the Lord, God shows us other issues that were not as apparent on the surface, such as selfishness, anger, and rebellion.

This reminds me of a powerful prophetic dream the Lord gave me several years ago. In the dream, my wife and I were halfway through a journey across the United States. Rather than stay at a hotel, we asked my former martial arts instructor if we could stay at his home for the night. He agreed, and when we arrived he said, "I'm going to show you the bedroom where you will be sleeping, but before I show you the bedroom, I want to show you this."

He promptly guided us upstairs to the bathroom and lifted the lid on the toilet so we could see into the bowl. It was filled with blue sanitizing fluid. Then my martial arts instructor, who stands about six-foot-three, suddenly dived into the toilet bowl and was shrunk down inside a translucent egg. I could see him inside the egg, surrounded by the blue sanitizing fluid, and he was joyful and content. A few seconds later he was standing beside us again, back in full stature and acting as if everything was normal.

He then showed us to the bedroom, and we went to sleep. The next morning my wife and I woke up, made the bed, and went downstairs. I said to my martial arts instructor, "We're on our way to continue the journey." To our surprise, he said, "Not so fast. Let's check the bedroom where you slept and make sure you're ready to leave." We went upstairs to the bedroom, and he began inspecting the room. He pulled a big dresser away from the wall, took out a toothbrush, and started scrubbing between the baseboard and the drywall. I was thinking, "What is he doing? Does he think we got it dirty down there? I mean, we only slept here one night."

He then reached behind the dresser, pulled out something that looked like an electrical box, and told me to set it up correctly. He went to the other side of the dresser, where an electrical wire was coming up from the floor. I had never seen anything like this. It was attached to the wall by what looked like telephone wire and appeared to have only a single button on top. So I "set it up" by doing the only thing I knew to do: I pushed the button.

"You're doing it wrong!" my teacher said. "You're not thinking. Here, let me show you." And with that he got down on his knees, grabbed the gadget, and flipped open a side panel I had not seen. Suddenly I could see that this gadget had many buttons inside. He entered a combination and reset the device, and then the dream ended.

I knew God was telling me something, so I asked Him to reveal the dream's meaning, and He began to show me what He was saying: "I want to cleanse you deeper than you realize right now. You thought you were done because you made the bed. You thought you were ready to move on in the journey, but I want to sanctify you. I want to sanitize you more deeply than you've been sanitized. You're not going to be able to continue on the journey into divine romance with Me until you let Me sanctify you at a deeper level."

The electrical cord with the gadget on the end represented my mind and thoughts. I had pushed a button without even thinking. The Lord was saying to me, "You're not examining your thoughts. I want you to start examining your thoughts because I want to sanctify your mind."

Father God certainly speaks to us powerfully through dreams, even if they are unusual! Maybe He has done the same for you.

Going deeper with Him in fellowship and divine romance involves addressing things inside us that we haven't considered before. This happens to each of us as we mature in our walk with God. We give up obvious vices first, and then the Holy Spirit turns the spotlight on our hearts to show us sin at even deeper levels. It's like looking through a magnifying glass at ten times the magnification, then cranking it up to a higher power. Previously unseen spots and blemishes will jump out at us!

But the Lord promises that "if we confess our sins, He is faithful and righteous to forgive us our sins and to cleanse us from all unrighteousness" (1 John 1:9). The Holy Spirit turns up the power of His light not to shame us but to show us what must be scrubbed out of our hearts and minds. This is Father God's mercy in action—He reveals our unrighteousness so we can be cleansed.

"I Have Not Kept My Vineyard"

The bride continues:

> My mother's sons were angry with me; they made me caretaker of the vineyards, but I have not taken care of my own vineyard.
>
> —SONG 1:6

As she confesses and describes realities in her walk with the King that are now apparent to her, she speaks about the oppression she has experienced in life. We see her in the midst of a mental struggle to retain the right perspective. She started the journey by encountering her Beloved, being kissed with the kisses of His mouth. She was so intoxicated with this experience that she said, "Draw me after you and let us run together." But as time went on, she ran smack-dab into some hard realities of life. Now she felt exposed to shame, and she recognized that others had treated her poorly, even as she tried to do the right things.

Many of us know what this feels like. Passionate about God, touched by the Lord, we start to run hard after Him—and then we find ourselves mired in the nitty-gritty of life, relationships, misunderstandings, and even betrayals. We work in the fields with the hot sun blazing on our backs. We walk through unpleasant family situations, financial troubles, and all sorts of circumstances that challenge our faith, joy, and peace. Over time these experiences seem to diminish the vibrant encounter we initially had with Yeshua. We struggle to hold on to the memories, and as with the bride in the Song, we start to lose our spiritual vitality.

It helps to see that the Shulamite maiden states three reasons for this dimming of the light inside her. First are her feelings of insecurity. Second are the responsibilities encroaching on her time to maintain communion with God. Third is the mistreatment she received from her "mother's sons."

Some of us can relate to this last one literally because we have been treated with disrespect by family members and others who should honor us. Perhaps a boss, coworkers, or family members want all your time and give very little in return. You get home from work and are met at the door with more responsibilities, complaints, and problems. It just seems sometimes that the people in your world don't appreciate you. You feel oppressed by circumstances and the people involved.

For some, mistreatment takes place in churches. Maybe the "mother's sons" in your community of believers have rejected you or treated you badly at times. Like the bride you feel burned and disconnected from God. You don't want anyone to look at you too closely because you feel insecure and unattractive. Worse, you may find yourself spending less time with the Lord, perhaps out of resentment that these things have happened. Whatever the case, the innocence and intimacy of the earlier encounters gave way to alienation and a sense of lifelessness in your spirit.

The truth is we all go through challenges like these, but with Messiah Jesus there is always a way out—and it starts by reconnecting to His emotions for us.

He Loves Us Already

Jesus said in John 17:26, "And I have made Your name known to them [my disciples], and will make it known, so that the love with which You loved Me may be in them, and I in them."

The first key to the Shulamite surviving and even thriving through this difficult part of the journey is the word *lovely* in verse 5 of chapter 1: "I am dark but *lovely*" (emphasis added). Yes, she is dark and imperfect, but she knows and declares that she is still lovely to God. This is a truly amazing moment in her life. Somehow, while being battered by these negative forces, she does not give up hope. She strengthens herself with the memory of past encounters and says none of the things happening to her have diminished the Lord's love for her. Wow!

Yes, Yeshua is cleansing us from some ugly things. Yes, there are plenty of issues we need to overcome—but our Beloved loves us right now. Each one of us is beautiful to Him. Each of us can confess with the Shulamite bride, "I am dark but lovely. Father God loves me right now, with everything that's going on. Praise the name of the Lord."

It's worth repeating the timeworn but true phrase: God will never love us more than He does right now. Even Paul, the "chief of sinners," said, "But thanks be to God, who always leads us in triumph in Christ" (2 Cor. 2:14). You see, the Lord has removed the sin factor from His assessment of us. Romans 8:1–4 tells us:

> Therefore there is now no condemnation for those who are in Christ Jesus. For the law of the Spirit of life in Christ Jesus has set you free from the law of sin and of death. For what the Law could not do, weak as it was through the flesh, God did: sending His own Son in the likeness of sinful flesh and as an offering for sin, He condemned sin in the flesh, so that the requirement of the Law might be fulfilled in us, who do not walk according to the flesh but according to the Spirit.

Because Jesus' blood has removed the blot of sin, the Bible says we stand before God holy and blameless, even in our worst times. We need to remind ourselves and one another that despite the sin the Holy Spirit brings to the surface in our lives, we are still lovely to God. We can boldly declare to our beloved Savior: "I am dark but lovely. I am beautiful to You. You created me in Your own image. David said in Psalm 139 that I am fearfully and wonderfully made. Second Corinthians 5:21 says that through Yeshua I have been made the righteousness of God. I am a new creation in Jesus, and God's Spirit is in me. The love of God has been shed abroad in my heart!"

Beloved one, we are lovely because we are created in God's image! We are lovely because He who knew no sin became sin on our behalf. So God looks at us through the eyes of the lovely One, Messiah Yeshua. Truly, our beauty is in the eyes of the Beholder. Yes, it may seem we become darker in our own eyes as the Lord reveals selfishness, pettiness, fear, and all those other things that don't benefit us. But His cleansing ultimately makes His mercy and perfect love shine brighter in and through us. "Mercy triumphs over judgment" (Jas. 2:13). We are indeed lovely to God.

Weak Yet Authentic Love

In the journey of divine love, everything—both the positive and the seemingly negative—should take us toward Jesus, not away from Him. The revelation of the sinfulness of her own heart pushed the Shulamite bride toward the Bridegroom rather than away from Him. Instead of fleeing, she called out to Him:

> Tell me, O you whom my soul loves, where do you pas-
> ture your flock.
>
> —Song 1:7

Notice again that though she is sunburned and imperfect, though she has neglected to take care of her vineyard, though others have mistreated her, still she does not see herself as disqualified. She doesn't consider herself a hopeless hypocrite or a reject. Rather, she calls out as one who has lost her way a little but maintains confidence that her Beloved will answer and help her.

She knew the character of her Beloved, that His heart is always to restore the repentant one, not cast him away. So she could ask confidently, "Where do You pasture Your flock? Where is Your presence abiding? How can I find You again? How can I reconnect? I don't want to be like a stranger to You. I don't want to feel disconnected from You anymore."

I think of Peter denying Jesus three times the night before Yeshua suffered the agony of the crucifixion. Messiah Jesus knew Peter was going to betray Him even back when He said to Peter, "Upon this rock I will build My church." (See Matthew 16:18.) Still, He chose Peter to be one of the pillars of the New Testament church and one of the writers of the Brit Hadashah, the New Testament.

The point is that Jesus didn't define Peter by his worst moment. Jesus saw clearly that Peter's love was weak but genuine. Yeshua said, "But I have prayed for you, that your faith may not fail; and you, when once you have turned again, strengthen your brothers" (Luke 22:32). Like Peter and the

Shulamite bride, just because your love is weak doesn't mean you are a hypocrite. Your love may be weak, but it's still authentic. It is still beautiful to God. So we must cry out in our moments of trouble, "O you whom my soul loves, where do you pasture your flock?"

Let me ask, Where do you go when you find yourself like this maiden—having had an encounter with Jesus, having tasted the goodness of His Word, but now feeling distant from Him? Your heart is not beating after Him as fast as it used to. You've lost something special in the relationship. You might even be lukewarm. What should you do? The same thing the Shulamite bride did. Call out to Him. Tell Him you want to sit under the protective presence of His shade tree again and that you yearn to experience His rest anew. Ask Him in repentance and love to draw you back.

When we seek to reconnect with our Beloved during the trials of life, He will not reject us. We naturally think He might come with a rebuke: "Why didn't you keep up your relationship with Me? Why did you let your vineyard disintegrate? Why did you let your fellowship with Me grow cold?" Instead, He comes as He did to the Shulamite bride, speaking love and acceptance, wiping away the shame and guilt she was feeling. He speaks tenderly and softly to us.

When he failed the Lord, Peter went away and wept bitterly. He was so ashamed that he felt unworthy to be an apostle anymore. Instead, he said, "I am going fishing" (John 21:3). Why would he go fishing? He wasn't taking a vacation to get his mind off things. He was returning to his former vocation as a fisherman because he felt he was no longer worthy to be an apostle of Yeshua.

What did Messiah Jesus do? He went to Peter in his place of shame and said, "'Simon, son of John, do you love Me more than these?' [Peter] said to Him, 'Yes, Lord; You know that I love You.' [Jesus] said to him, 'Tend My lambs.'

"[Jesus] said to him again a second time, 'Simon, son of John, do you love Me?' [Peter said again], 'Yes, Lord; You know that I love You.' He said to him, 'Shepherd My sheep.'

"[Yeshua] said to him the third time, 'Simon, son of John, do you love Me?' Peter was grieved because He said to him the third time, 'Do you love Me?' And he said to Him, 'Lord, You know all things; You know that I love You.' Jesus said to him, 'Tend My sheep'" (John 21:15–17).

You see, Jesus was restoring Peter to his place of intimacy. He was saying, "Run with Me again. I don't reject you. Let's be near each other as we were before—and even closer. Let's work side by side." Yeshua even made Peter declare his love three times to override the three times Peter denied Him. He was building strength back into this leader of the church. Jesus was resolidifying Peter's heart in His love.

Beloved one, let this truth settle deep in your heart as you proclaim this revelation now.

> *Lord Jesus, I affirm and agree that I am beautiful to You. You are my beautiful Bridegroom King, and You created me in Your image. You took away my sin and made me Your righteousness. I stand before You holy and blameless right now. Thank You that I am pleasing to You, and help me to understand even more how beautiful I am to You and how beautiful You are. Thank You, Lord Jesus, for purchasing me*

with Your own blood and making me lovely. Help me to go deep into Your grace and experience the mystery of Your love. Hallelujah!

Chapter 5

WHERE DO YOU PASTURE YOUR FLOCK?

THE SHULAMITE BRIDE then asks her Beloved:

For why should I be like one who veils herself beside the flocks of your companions?

—SONG 1:7

In the ancient world a woman would veil herself when working in the company of strangers. She didn't veil herself when she was at home or with familiar friends. So in verse 7 she was asking her Bridegroom: "Why should I be like a stranger to You? Why should I be like one who veils herself? Why must there be this distance between us?" In our day we might say, "I don't want just to be with Your friends. I want to be with You myself!"

Find Fellowship

Jesus gives her a beautiful response, and He does the same for us as we cry out to Him. He begins by saying,

> If you yourself do not know, most beautiful among women...
>
> —Song 1:8

I have to pause here and say, Isn't it magnificent the way He treats her—and us? The Shulamite bride was once passionate about the King; she had encountered the kisses of His Word and had been brought into the bridal chamber. But through the stresses and responsibilities of life, her love had begun to grow cold. She was sensing a distance between her and the Bridegroom, and she wanted to find her way back to His presence. She'd felt the fire of His love on her heart, and she wanted that closeness back.

Instead of making her feel ashamed or rejected, He calls her the "most beautiful among women." Some would say, "This woman is a hypocrite! She said she wanted to be close to the Bridegroom yet neglected their relationship." But a hypocrite is not somebody who says one thing and does another. If that were the case, every one of us would be a hypocrite. For example, how many of us have said we were going on a diet and then ate unhealthy foods? How many of us have pledged never to commit a particular sin again and then fell back into old patterns? No, a hypocrite is someone who says he is going to do something but never has a real intention of doing it. He is a liar who hides that fact from others. A hypocrite's heart isn't in alignment with what he says. Jesus does not overlook true hypocrisy, but neither does He label us "hypocrites" when we sincerely try to reach the mark and fall short.

Yeshua gives the maiden profound counsel about how to reconnect with Him, expressed in the natural language of her day, when He answers her question by saying:

> Go forth on the trail of the flock.
>
> —SONG 1:8

His counsel is essentially, "Find others who are following Me. Get into fellowship with them." I have watched too many Christians drop out of fellowship altogether because they got burned by an experience at church or hurt by a Christian brother or sister. A single incident made them angry and distrustful of Christians. Others simply got busy and stopped attending church regularly. They didn't prioritize staying connected with the body of believers. For whatever reason, there are far too many professing Christians who don't go to church and forsake the assembling together with the believing community. They live separated from the body of Messiah. Yeshua says to such people, "If you want to be close to Me, You've got to get into fellowship with My people. Start by gathering again with My flock."

A lot of people don't like to hear that. They want to go through life, just them and Jesus. But spiritual solitude is not permitted in God's family. We must humble ourselves and gather with others who believe the gospel.

The Bible says in Hebrews 10:24–25:

> And let us consider how to stimulate one another to
> love and good deeds, not forsaking our own assembling

together, as is the habit of some, but encouraging one another; and all the more as you see the day drawing near.

The Christian life does not really exist without sincere, loving relationships. It would be a loveless faith, which is no faith at all. If Yeshua's love is in us, then it needs to be displayed not only in our relationship with Him but in the way we relate to—and enjoy and forgive and encourage and love—other people.

I give you a tender warning now: if you are in good health and not attending church anywhere, your lack of fellowship will hamper your relationship with God. To participate fully in the life of Yeshua, we must live in relationship with other people. Messiah Jesus prayed in John 17 that His people would be one, even as He is one with the Father. Notice this is a group endeavor, not a program for lone rangers.

The enemy is the one who divides and isolates. God always unites and draws people together. In fact, the promises of God in the New Testament are usually given as corporate promises, not individual ones. They are given to a body of people. Paul never conceived of individual Christians pursuing their faith journeys alone. Rather, he spent a lot of time teaching local groups of Christians how to get along with one another. Take a look at just some of the things he wrote, encouraging unity and peace:

> Now I urge you, brethren, keep your eye on those who cause dissensions and hindrances contrary to the teaching which you learned, and turn away from them. For such men are slaves, not of our Lord Christ but of their own

appetites; and by their smooth and flattering speech they deceive the hearts of the unsuspecting. For the report of your obedience has reached to all; therefore I am rejoicing over you, but I want you to be wise in what is good and innocent in what is evil. The God of peace will soon crush Satan under your feet.

—Romans 16:17–20

For just as we have many members in one body and all the members do not have the same function, so we, who are many, are one body in Christ, and individually members one of another. Since we have gifts that differ according to the grace given to us, each of us is to exercise them accordingly: if prophecy, according to the proportion of his faith; if service, in his serving; or he who teaches, in his teaching; or he who exhorts, in his exhortation; he who gives, with liberality; he who leads, with diligence; he who shows mercy, with cheerfulness....

Be devoted to one another in brotherly love; give preference to one another in honor; not lagging behind in diligence, fervent in spirit, serving the Lord; rejoicing in hope, persevering in tribulation, devoted to prayer, contributing to the needs of the saints, practicing hospitality. Bless those who persecute you; bless and do not curse. Rejoice with those who rejoice, and weep with those who weep. Be of the same mind toward one another; do not be haughty in mind, but associate with the lowly. Do not be wise in your own estimation. Never pay back evil for evil to anyone. Respect what is right in the sight of all men. If possible, so far as it depends on you, be at peace with all men.

—Romans 12:4–18

> Always seek after that which is good for one another and for all people.
>
> —1 Thessalonians 5:15

> For even as the body is one and yet has many members, and all the members of the body, though they are many, are one body, so also is Christ. For by one Spirit we were all baptized into one body, whether Jews or Greeks, whether slaves or free, and we were all made to drink of one Spirit. For the body is not one member, but many. If the foot says, "Because I am not a hand, I am not a part of the body," it is not for this reason any the less a part of the body. And if the ear says, "Because I am not an eye, I am not a part of the body," it is not for this reason any the less a part of the body. If the whole body were an eye, where would the hearing be? If the whole were hearing, where would the sense of smell be? But now God has placed the members, each one of them, in the body, just as He desired. If they were all one member, where would the body be? But now there are many members, but one body....And if one member suffers, all the members suffer with it; if one member is honored, all the members rejoice with it. Now you are Christ's body, and individually members of it.
>
> —1 Corinthians 12:12–20, 26–27

In other words, we all need to be connected to one another, though we differ significantly. None of us are islands unto ourselves. We are each called to be a part of Jesus' body. So the first thing Yeshua says to the Shulamite bride when she expresses her desire to be closer to Him is to get into fellowship and relationship with the rest of His people.

I understand that some cannot leave home to attend church or are bedbound, and I would like to pray for you.

> *Father, I pray for these who are homebound. Refresh them, bless them, let them experience Your love, and bring them into the fellowship with others that You have ordained for them.*

Pasture Your Goats

In telling the maiden how she can reconnect with Him, the Bridegroom then says:

> And *pasture your young goats* by the tents of the shepherds.
>
> —Song 1:8, emphasis added

So in verse 8 He first points the bride to a place ("on the trail of the flock," or in fellowship with other believers) and then to a task ("pasture your young goats"). Through this He is telling us, "Get involved in service again." We are to imitate Yeshua, who came as a servant and in John 13 stooped down, girded Himself with a towel, and washed the disciples' feet. This will always be His nature. If we want to experience His presence, we need to serve alongside Him. His Spirit flows in the direction of serving. Messiah Jesus said, "But the greatest among you shall be your servant" (Matt. 23:11).

Where do we pasture our "young goats"? He tells us to do it specifically "by the tents of the shepherds." These represent God-instituted authorities. This means we must learn how to relate to the authorities and authority structures God has put in place on the earth. We all know authority requires order.

Without authority there is chaos. God has anointed "shepherds" in various spheres of life—from families to churches to municipalities to nations. All authority is God's authority, and Father God vests His authority in human beings on the earth. He expects us to relate to and respect this authority as unto Him. We are submitting to God when we submit to the authority He has delegated to other people. So the Lord is telling the Shulamite bride, "Go get under the authority of My leaders."

We live in a society today where men and women are throwing off authority. Some of it is plain rebellion, but some of it is a reaction to the misuse of authority. Again, people cry, "Hypocrites!" And they remove themselves from the "tents of the shepherds." But God never said He would only vest authority in perfect people—because there are no perfect people. Those in authority have flaws just like the rest of humanity. For instance, nobody on a police force is perfect, but if there were no police force, chaos and crime would reign.

Moses was not a perfect leader. He got angry and struck a rock in direct disobedience to what God told him to do. Earlier, when Father God called him to lead the Hebrew nation, Moses argued with Him and tried to get out of the assignment, and God actually became angry with him! Moses was far from perfect, yet God chose him. Interestingly, a time came when many in the congregation of Israel said to Moses, and I paraphrase, "Who do you think you are, leading us like you're the only one capable of making these decisions? We're all holy, not just you." Whether they realized it or not, they were throwing off God's authority, and the threat of anarchy and chaos became very real because everyone was going to become a law unto himself.

Moses, like a good shepherd, fell on his face and asked God what he should do. The Lord told him that each tribe was to lay out a rod, and the rod God caused to supernaturally bud would prove which person He had chosen to exercise His authority. Aaron's rod budded. God made it plain that not everybody is chosen to be in authority, and the ground opened up and swallowed those who rebelled! (See Numbers 16 and 17.)

There is no functioning kingdom without authority. Messiah Jesus came to institute the kingdom of God with all its authority. To walk closely with Yeshua, we must get back into fellowship with His people, serve in His "flock," and remain under the authority of the shepherds who oversee His local churches. This does not mean giving them complete control over our lives but rather submitting to their decision-making in the context of that body of believers. Remember, no one in authority will be perfect, but we need to respect God's authority by respecting His shepherds and leaders.

The apostle Paul put it this way:

> But we request of you, brethren, that you appreciate those who diligently labor among you, and have charge over you in the Lord and give you instruction, and that you esteem them very highly in love because of their work. Live in peace with one another.
>
> —1 Thessalonians 5:12–13

He also wrote this to the believers in Rome:

Every person is to be in subjection to the governing authorities. For there is no authority except from God, and those which exist are established by God. Therefore whoever resists authority has opposed the ordinance of God; and they who have opposed will receive condemnation upon themselves. For rulers are not a cause of fear for good behavior, but for evil. Do you want to have no fear of authority? Do what is good and you will have praise from the same; for it is a minister of God to you for good. But if you do what is evil, be afraid; for it does not bear the sword for nothing; for it is a minister of God, an avenger who brings wrath on the one who practices evil. Therefore it is necessary to be in subjection, not only because of wrath, but also for conscience' sake.

—ROMANS 13:1–5

As Paul urged, we should love and pray for those called to lead. God is not pleased when we go about criticizing, gossiping, and tearing down our leaders. This includes ripping up their sermons on the way home or at the restaurant after church! We need to bless those who carry the weight of God's authority in our communities. I know they are human beings, but by honoring the authority God has invested in them, we honor God.

To recap once again, the Shulamite bride had been exposed to the Bridegroom, and she opened her heart and developed a passionate, fiery love for Him. She said, "Kiss me with the kisses of Your Word. Draw me after You, and let us run this race together on earth." But over time the stresses of life and the darkness in this world caused her to feel a loss of intimacy. So she cried out, "Where are You? I don't want to feel like a stranger to You. How can I reconnect with You?" Yeshua responded by saying: "Oh, you whom My soul loves, get back in fellowship with My people, look for ways to serve, and learn to come under the authority of the shepherds I have put in place."

Just as it was for the Shulamite woman, when we practice those three principles, God will strengthen us and bring us into deeper oneness with Him. Let's set our hearts to walk in fellowship with others, find life-giving places to serve, and render honor to those who have been placed in authority.

I encourage you to invite the Holy Spirit to make these keys a reality in your life.

> *Lord Jesus, I resist the root of bitterness that would keep me from joyful fellowship with the body of believers. I admit it if I have isolated myself from others, separating myself from the nourishment, comfort, and strength of the body. Help me to forgive those who have hurt me so we can be one as You and the Father are one.*
>
> *Yeshua, make me a servant, as You Yourself came as a servant, and help me to respect the authorities You have put in place in the earth and in so doing honor You.*
>
> *Father, I thank You for the relationships You have given me to enjoy. I love Your leadership over me and over Your body.*

Chapter 6

THE PRAISE OF THE BRIDEGROOM

ESSIAH JESUS CONTINUES to speak to the maiden, affirming her and wooing her back to Himself. He says, "To me, my darling, you are like..." (Song 1:9), and then He lists the qualities He sees in her that bless Him.

Beloved, the Lord doesn't see you the way you see yourself, or the way others see you. He doesn't define us by our failures or our struggles. He sees our eternal identities and destinies—who we are in Him and who He has called us to become. He praises us for qualities we don't even know we possess. God wants you to know that you are His best. You are His favorite. Others can be God's best and His favorite too, but that doesn't take away from the fact that you are uniquely His best, His favorite, His most beautiful. That's the way God feels about all of us, and He wants us to have that revelation in our own hearts. Jesus didn't just die for the world; He died for you, personally. That's a big deal.

He goes on to say the Shulamite bride is like

...my mare among the chariots of Pharaoh.

—SONG 1:9

The chariots of Pharaoh were led by the mightiest and most expensive horses on the planet. They were warhorses that represented dominating strength and beauty. In making this comparison, the Bridegroom was telling her, "I see strength in you. But you are more than just strong; you have the heart of a warrior and an overcomer." Our King Jesus sees the same qualities in us even when we don't see them. Through the Song, He is expressing, "I see strength in you, like a battle-tested horse. I see in you a victorious overcomer. You are indeed royal to Me, and you are destined to reign with Me for all eternity. You are the best." Wow!

As the Bridegroom reveals this to her, it touches her heart and floods her with revelation. Her view of herself radically shifts to come into alignment with His. Enraptured by her grace and potential to conquer, He continues in verse 10 by saying:

Your cheeks are lovely with ornaments.

Cheeks represent and reveal emotions. When you smile, your cheeks reflect your mood. When you frown, they take on a different expression. Our emotions are important to Him. Yeshua Himself has emotions, and He responds to our feelings.

They are not ugly, embarrassing, or emblematic of weakness. Rather, our emotions in Him adorn us like lovely ornaments.

The Bridegroom then finishes the verse by poetically describing His bride's royalty in this way:

> ...your neck with strings of beads.
>
> —Song 1:10

He is speaking here about the maiden's aristocracy. We are priests and children of God who have been called to sit with Messiah Jesus in the heavenly places in royalty forever. Notice what the Bridegroom says next in verse 11:

> We will make for you ornaments of gold with beads of silver.

What does this mean? First, note the use of the word *we.* Yeshua is saying the Father, Son, and Holy Spirit together as one are going to complete in you what they started. They have a perfect plan to bring your life to its highest fulfillment. There is a call on you to forever be conformed to God's image, and the Father, Son, and Holy Spirit are working together now to accomplish that.

"Gold" refers to the character of God and the quality of God's nature throughout the Tanakh, or the Hebrew Bible. "Beads of silver" represent the redemption we have in Yeshua. So the Lord is saying to her, "I am going to make you like Me. By the time I'm done, you're going to shine like gold that has been refined in fire because of My redeeming work in your life." And though He is not finished with this sanctifying work in your life, He loves you and is moved by you right now.

Secure in Him, Our Hearts Open Up

After Yeshua tells the Shulamite bride, "I'm going to complete what I started in you. I'm going to make you like gold. You are royal to Me, and you're going to reign in the heavenly places with Me," she replies by saying:

> While the king was at his table, my *perfume* gave forth its fragrance.
>
> —Song 1:12, emphasis added

When her Beloved spoke to her, her heart opened back up to Him and gave forth a rare perfume. This happened as she became convinced of how beautiful she was to him. As you and I become convinced of how much God loves us, our hearts open up to Him in this same way. We become secure. We begin to trust Him. The true nature of who we are unfolds to Him like an aromatic flower. That is what happens in the Shulamite bride's life. She opens up and becomes the person she truly is as she is made to feel secure in the love of God.

The Book of 2 Corinthians speaks about the fragrance of the Lord in a passage I referenced earlier:

> But thanks be to God, who always leads us in triumph in Christ, and manifests through us the sweet *aroma* of the knowledge of Him in every place. For we are a *fragrance* of Christ to God among those who are being saved and among those who are perishing; to the one an aroma from death to death, to the other an aroma from life to life.
>
> —2 Corinthians 2:14–16, emphasis added

If we are a fragrance to God, what is that fragrance? Paul says it is a fragrance "of Christ." I said earlier that fragrances represent true inner attributes. Even as the internal chemicals and properties in the flower are manifested by its fragrance, so each one of us gives forth the "fragrance" of our character. For believers, that fragrance is "of Christ." The beauty of Yeshua is inside us. What an incredible reality that when Father God "smells" us, He smells the essence, the fragrance, the purity, the freshness, and the beauty of Christ emanating from our innermost beings. I'd rather smell like Him than like me!

The Sweetness and Bitterness of Myrrh

Remember, this love song is a duet, and so she now responds:

> My beloved is to me a pouch of myrrh which lies all night between my breasts.
>
> —Song 1:13

Myrrh has multiple and complex characteristics. It smells sweet but tastes bitter. In Matthew 2:11, the wise men presented myrrh to Jesus when He was born. Myrrh also was used to anoint people for burial. (See John 19:39–40.) When the wise men presented the gift of myrrh at Yeshua's birth, they were saying how beautiful and fragrant He was, but they were also participating in a prophetic promise of the gift Jesus would give to the world in His death.

What is the prophetic meaning here of the maiden holding myrrh on her bosom? The bride was conveying, "I hold my Jesus close to me all night, and I remember that He loves me so much that He died for me." This is a good habit for us to have: When you lie in bed at night, think about Messiah Jesus and His extravagant gift of love for us. Hold on to it when you are going through difficult times in the "night seasons" of life. When God seems far away, hold the memory of Him in that place close to your heart all night long. It will help you go safely through the trial.

The maiden continues to extol the beauty of her Bridegroom, saying,

> My beloved is to me a cluster of henna blossoms in the vineyard of Engedi.
>
> —Song 1:14

Engedi is a beautiful place in Israel with many fragrances and flowers. The bride makes reference to the multiplied pleasures of Engedi by noting that her Beloved is to her "a cluster of henna blossoms"—not just one blossom but many. Broadly speaking, the beauty of creation radiates countless facets of Yeshua's beauty, from the awesome height and majesty of great mountains to the preciousness of something small, like newborn babies or puppies. Flowers, oceans, horses, the sky—all are part of the manifold beauty of God.

I recently had an encounter with God that was so powerful and breathtaking I literally felt like I couldn't breathe. In this encounter, I experienced God's beauty manifesting as living color. When I saw it, I felt as though I couldn't breathe because it was so other, so holy, so powerful and beautiful that my flesh could not exist in its presence. When I saw Him, I felt like John in Revelation 1:17, who "fell at His feet like a dead man." Beloved, this living being of color and beauty that I encountered was so extreme that it left me in awe and aware of how great and terrible He is, in the most wonderful way.

God has made His invisible beauty manifest to us in the natural world. "For since the creation of the world His invisible attributes, His eternal power and divine nature, have been clearly seen, being understood through what has been made" (Rom. 1:20).

Some of us get disconnected from the beauty of God all around us because we are so connected to our cell phones and computers. We need to recognize the "cluster of henna blossoms" multiplied a million times in God's beautiful creation. God is beauty, and His creation reflects that.

Eyes Like Doves

The dialogue in the Song continues with Jesus, the Bridegroom, saying:

> How beautiful you are, my darling, how beautiful you are! Your eyes are like doves.
>
> —Song 1:15

There is a reason the Holy Spirit, the Ruach HaKodesh, descended as a dove during Yeshua's baptism (Luke 3:21–22). God made doves with characteristics that speak of His Spirit's attributes. For example, one of the unique facts about doves is that they can only see straight ahead. Messiah Jesus was telling the maiden at this point in her journey into divine love, "Nothing to the right or left distracts you. Like a dove, your eyes are fixed ahead, focused on Me and My direction alone. That is beautiful."

The other wonderful thing about doves is that they mate

once for life. If the spouse dies, the partner never "marries" again. So it is with each one of us who has committed our lives to Jesus. We are to be like doves in our loyalty to Him. Yeshua was saying to the bride, "You have become so loyal to me now. Our eyes are fixed on each other, and we are walking in marital intimacy."

Doves are also affectionate. The one thing Jesus desires that nobody can give Him but you is your affection. He desires this more than anything. He calls us to become like the Shulamite bride and make Him the true love of our lives. We are to be like the merchant Yeshua spoke of who went and sold everything he had to buy the pearl of great price.

> Again, the kingdom of heaven is like a merchant seeking fine pearls, and upon finding one pearl of great value, he went and sold all that he had and bought it.
> —MATTHEW 13:45–46

Jesus is our pearl of great price, worth everything we have.

The Green Couch

In Song 1:16 the maiden again speaks, saying, "How handsome you are, my beloved, and so pleasant! Indeed, our couch is luxuriant," or "green," as the King James Version translates it. This describes the bridal couch on which the King and His bride were carried to the wedding.

The couch or bed speaks of the rest and comfort the bride has with her lover, Jesus. She feels safe and alive in Him. We too can experience this rest in Messiah Jesus. Yeshua said, "Come to Me, all who are weary and heavy-laden, and I will give you rest. Take My yoke upon you and learn from Me, for

I am gentle and humble in heart, and you will find rest for your souls. For My yoke is easy and My burden is light" (Matt. 11:28–30).

We enter this rest when we realize King Jesus has authority over all the circumstances of our lives. This knowledge gives us a deep sense of assurance in the midst of our trials. When we are resting on the bridal couch with King Jesus, nothing shakes our confidence because we know that no matter what happens, He is in control.

The maiden describes the couch as "luxuriant" or "green," which means her life is full and fruitful. When something is green, that's a sign it is alive and growing. Jesus said He came to give life and to give it more abundantly—that is a promise for us personally to apprehend. As we journey with Yeshua, we find our lives becoming far more dynamic and productive— "luxuriant" and "green."

The maiden goes on to say in verse 17, "The beams of our houses are cedars, our rafters, cypresses." Cedar was the strongest, most expensive building material known to man back then. For example, it was used to construct the temple. In this we see that the internal foundations our Bridegroom lays inside us are unshakeable, made of the most durable substances; they cannot be washed away. Yeshua explained this in a parable.

> Therefore everyone who hears these words of Mine and acts on them, may be compared to a wise man who built his house on the rock. And the rain fell, and the floods came, and the winds blew and slammed against that house; and yet it did not fall, for it had been founded on the rock. Everyone who hears these words of Mine and

does not act on them, will be like a foolish man who built his house on the sand. The rain fell, and the floods came, and the winds blew and slammed against that house; and it fell—and great was its fall.

—MATTHEW 7:24–27

What our lives are built on matters! When Messiah Jesus is our foundation, we don't collapse when trials and tribulations come—we stand strong. Life's challenges reveal what we're made of. When our beams aren't "cedar" and our rafters not "cypress," our houses are like the one built on sand. When life suddenly changes and we lose a job or suffer health problems, or a loved one passes away, we collapse. Much better to make Yeshua our foundation and build our lives in Him! As we do, Father God builds something rich and powerful in us that nothing can overturn.

The Rose of Sharon

The Shulamite bride begins to feel this, so she declares as we enter chapter 2, "I am the rose of Sharon, the lily of the valleys" (v. 1).

Does this sound strange to you? Do you ever verbally affirm your own beauty to God? To some—maybe you—this is a foreign concept. You wouldn't think of praising yourself with words of affirmation, perhaps because it strikes you as prideful; or maybe you simply don't believe in your own loveliness to God. Yet speaking God's perspective of things out loud is one of the most powerful and important things we can do. It is also one of the greatest ways to come into our true identity.

We need to break Satan's shame and guilt from our lives, and words act like a sledgehammer, breaking up false ideas and strongholds of lies. We are the children of a beautiful God. John said, "See how great a love the Father has bestowed on us, that we would be called children of God; and such we are" (1 John 3:1). The bride's statement about being "the rose of Sharon," the flower of love, invites us likewise to say of ourselves, "I am beautiful and attractive to God, just like the very best things He has made in creation. I look good; I smell good—He likes me!"

She also mentions the lily, a flower that represents purity and obedience. This is why we say something is "lily white." In our day the standard for purity is quite polluted. We live in a world where Satan tells Christians it's OK to live in immorality and compromise. "Everybody else is doing it," he says. "It's just a normal part of today's society."

Speaking of this delusion, God's Word says, "When they measure themselves by themselves...they are without understanding" (2 Cor. 10:12). The world is rife with impurity and defilement. This is especially so in relation to sexual sin. God's standard has not changed with a changing world.

Consider that God's Word teaches that sexual sin is closely connected to the inner man. It is actually more defiling than other sins. Paul put it this way:

> Flee immorality. Every other sin that a man commits is outside the body, but the immoral man sins against his own body. Or do you not know that your body is a temple of the Holy Spirit who is in you, whom you have from God, and that you are not your own? For you have

been bought with a price: therefore glorify God in your body.

—1 CORINTHIANS 6:18–20

Jesus calls you and me to be "lilies," to live in sexual purity. If you are not living in sexual purity, I challenge you to recognize how serious a matter this is. Your Lord is a jealous God and will not share you with another. If you persist in impurity as a child of God, He will discipline you, and it may cost you much. It will hurt. He is not rejecting you. He disciplines us to correct us because He loves us. It's a rescue operation!

But the Bible offers a less painful and less costly solution; it says we have the opportunity to examine ourselves and repent, and thereby escape the pain of being disciplined by God. Paul wrote:

But if we judged ourselves rightly, we would not be judged. But when we are judged, we are disciplined by the Lord so that we will not be condemned along with the world.

—1 CORINTHIANS 11:31–32

None of us can enter the depths of knowing God without repenting. If you are living in disobedience, it means your relationship with Yeshua lacks depth. It is not growing, and in fact it is going backward. Repent from sin and turn to Him! Confess to Him that by His strength you will live as a lily of the valley. It doesn't matter what the world does. It doesn't matter what the world says. You have been called to be a pure and undefiled bride to Him. You and I can declare with the

Shulamite bride, who is a shadow of the church, "I am the rose of Sharon, the lily of the valleys."

The Song continues, "Like a lily among the thorns, so is my darling among the maidens" (Song 2:2). Though surrounded by darkness and "thorns," we are still called to live as lilies.

Take this revelation to the Lord in prayer:

> *Lord Jesus, thank You for giving me eyes like a dove— of loyalty and single focus. Strengthen my eyes and my devotion to You. Thank You also that You see me as strong, as a warrior, that You are building in me a firm foundation I can rest in with complete assurance. Thank You that You have made me lovely and pure, that though I currently live in the valley among thorns in this fallen age, You empower me to live rightly before Your eyes. Father, I ask You to strengthen me to grow even more in purity. Amen and amen.*

Chapter 7

HIS BANNER OF LOVE OVER YOU

I LOVE THE BACK-AND-FORTH dialogue throughout the Song. It invites us again to speak to Jesus while reading. Remember, the Song is given as our own personal, divinely inspired conversation with Yeshua. We declare who He is and who we are in Him. He agrees with us, whispering to our spirits the same wonderful truths the King spoke to the Shulamite bride.

Chapter 2 of the Song continues with the maiden saying, "Like an apple tree among the trees of the forest, so is my beloved among the young men....Refresh me with apples, because I am lovesick" (vv. 3, 5).

A scene unfolds before the eyes of our heart now. The Shulamite bride is strolling through the forest when she comes upon an apple tree. Pine and other forest trees are nice and provide great shade and scent, but they don't provide fruit that refreshes us. The apple tree does, however, and she immediately compares it to her lover as her source of satisfaction and life.

This kind of provision is worth stopping for and glorifying in, so she exults, "In his shade I took great delight and sat down." She paused to be refreshed. It reminds me of Mary the sister of Lazarus in Luke 10. She sat down at Jesus' feet and received from Him as He was ministering. She put other things aside. She didn't just pass by the apple tree in the forest. Instead, she sat down and took great delight in what it offered.

So is our relationship with Messiah Jesus. We can pass by if we're not careful to develop our sense of His presence, but let's make Him our first love and take time to stop and sit in His shade. Like the Shulamite bride, we discover day after day that "his fruit was sweet to my taste."

Marking Moments

This exquisite moment in the forest marks the bride forever. It is comparable to those significant encounters in life that propel us forward and are indelibly written onto our hearts and memories. Not every day is spectacular. Much of the time it's a simple walk in the forest—nothing unusual or extravagant. No surprises. But over the course of our journeys as children of God, there are marking moments in space and time on this earth when Yeshua reveals Himself to us in a deeply personal way. They touch us and change us for what is ahead.

These "markings" come in a million different ways. They can happen while we're reading the Word of God, watching a sunset, sitting quietly, or in a loud, exuberant worship service.

They may come out of the blue while we're driving some-where on a normal day. No matter how they happen, these moments elevate us. We experience the ineffable, intoxicating, rapturous presence of God in some unique way. The truth is that we need these marking encounters because people who have never encountered Jesus become easily bored with Christianity. "Apple tree moments" convince us anew that He is alive and active and cares for us personally. They spark in us a new passion to pursue Him.

The time spent under the apple tree leads to an even greater breakthrough. Over time the bride lost a sense of closeness. In that disconnected state, she called out, saying, "Help me to get back to You." Jesus responded to her and affirmed her, and her heart opened up to Him again. Now, in renewed pursuit of Him, she cries out,

> Sustain me with raisin cakes, refresh me with apples, because I am lovesick.
>
> —SONG 2:5

Have you ever loved someone so much that you felt pow-erless in his or her presence? You could hardly work because you couldn't stop thinking about this person. You wanted to be with him or her all the time. That is the condition of the bride here. She feels weak because she loves the Bridegroom so much. She is desperate to draw closer to him. In a word, she is lovesick and calls out to be sustained in this state of seeming helplessness.

Several years ago when I was ministering at a Messianic congregation I was leading in Ohio, I sensed in my heart that the Holy Spirit was doing a deep work in some people's lives.

I felt He was bringing them to a place of crossing over, like the children of Israel crossed the Jordan River. Afterward, the Israelites built a memorial to mark that something significant had happened; it was a place of remembrance of what the Lord had done. In a similar way I sensed the Lord was uprooting some things, setting people free and bringing them to a new state of closeness in their walk with Him.

I wasn't planning to do this, but at the end of the service I felt the unction of the Holy Spirit to invite forward those who felt this was happening in their lives. Fifteen people responded, and I had us hold hands in a circle. I took authority in the Spirit and drew a line, so to speak, and said, "A brand new thing has happened. God has brought you to a new place in Him, with a new ability to walk with Him, to experience His love and intimacy. As a result of this, He is going to sustain this new place with raisin cakes. Over the next weeks, God is going to sustain the commitment you have made with raisin cakes."

It was an unusual thing to say, except that "raisin cakes" was mentioned in the portion of Scripture I had been teaching from that morning. Of course, raisin cakes are literal foods made from dried grapes, but they are not very common anymore, at least not in the United States. But a few weeks later one of those fifteen people who had come forward approached me during a service and said, "I've got a testimony to share." I gave him permission to speak it to the congregation.

He told how after the "raisin cakes" service he was driving down the road and really struggling. He had health issues and other challenges. He prayed, "Lord, I thank You for all the things You have done for me. You don't have to do anything else for me. I know You want to teach me to live by faith and not by sight, but I'm really struggling right now. If You could do something—if You could give me a raisin cake to encourage me, refresh me, and let me know You're there—I would really appreciate it."

Right when he was praying, his phone rang. It was his wife. She said a particular Spirit-led person in their lives had visited. This person would mysteriously show up at strategic times to share encouraging words for them from the Lord. This woman had come over and left a bag with some items in it for the man. That lifted his spirits, and when he got home and opened the bag, he received an even bigger surprise. This woman, who was not part of our congregation and knew nothing about what had happened at church, had delivered a gift of raisin cakes. Jesus knew exactly how to let that man know, "I am sustaining your faith and refreshing you for the next phase of the journey."

That is what it's like feasting in the banquet hall of the Lord. He takes care of us!

The Banner Over Our Lives

That man in my congregation could attest to the Shulamite bride's words, "His banner over me is love." A banner is the regal flag that armies walk under in a time of war or during a drill or procession. It is the covering under which a tribe gathers. Banners proclaim identity, belonging, loyalty, and community principles.

The banner over our lives, as followers of Yeshua, is love. There is nothing higher than that. Messiah Jesus is leading us onward through various battles and is already victorious over everything on earth. We can trust Him to turn everything that happens to us for good: "And we know that God causes all things to work together for good to those who love God, to those who are called according to His purpose. For those whom He foreknew, He also predestined to become conformed to the image of His Son, so that He would be the firstborn among many brethren" (Rom. 8:28–29). His love overshadows us like a royal banner waving over our heads. Circumstances do not control us. The future cannot harm us. We have a King who cannot suffer defeat.

As a result of this, the maiden continues in Song 2:6, "Let his left hand be under my head and his right hand embrace me." Since the right hand of God represents His manifest power, perhaps the left hand of God here represents His unseen activity. She is saying, "Yeshua, sustain me in every area of my life with Your love, even in those areas where I can't discern You or Your workings." Think of how many things the Lord has done for us in His love that we have not perceived. Imagine how many accidents He has spared you from on the roadways, and you didn't even know it.

Day by day He strengthens us, though we don't realize He is doing it. He extinguishes germs we never even knew were there. Again and again, Yeshua's love has shepherded you into making right decisions, led you into right relationships, closed doors to protect you from bad situations, and opened doors to lead you into good ones. All this time you hardly perceived it was Him.

Several years back my wife and I were planning to move. We were living in a city about two and a half hours away from the Messianic congregation I was leading. I had been serving this congregation for ten years, ever since my children were still young and in school. I told the congregation many times over the years that when my children graduated from high school, my wife and I would move to the city where the congregation was located. It didn't make sense to be shepherding a congregation that was more than two hours from my house.

When my youngest daughter graduated from high school, my wife and I automatically began to look for houses close to the congregation. We found a particular home we liked and put a contract on it. Later that night, I went back to the house and sat on a little bench in the backyard.

"Father," I said, "is this the house You have for us?" Then I went back to the church building where I had a rabbi's quarters to sleep in when I was in town. I went to sleep and had a very brief vision of the night. The Holy Spirit showed me a picture of myself sitting on the same bench I had been sitting on hours earlier, but in the dream I wasn't just on a bench—I was in a stockade. A stockade is a wooden device where your neck and wrists are trapped; it holds you prisoner. It was a powerful and troubling image, and far outside my ordinary experience or imagination. I knew it was coming from the Holy Spirit and that the Lord was telling me, "Don't buy this house. If you buy this house, you are going to be trapped." I didn't understand why; I just understood that the Holy Spirit was telling me not to do it.

Later, when the seller made a counteroffer, I just let the deal die. I knew God was telling me, "Don't buy that house." I didn't know if the Lord was telling me not to buy *that* house or if He was telling me not to move to the area at all, so I prayed, "Lord, I'm going to look for another house to see if

You were just telling us not to move to this specific house or not to move to this city at all." So my wife and I found another house, and it seemed ideal for our future. It was in the price range we wanted, and it had the features we were looking for. It had been on the market for a year and a half, so we felt confident this was going to be the home we would purchase. I put the offer in on a Friday.

On Monday I got a call from the real estate agent. Somebody had bought that house over the internet for full asking price, sight unseen. I thought, "Lord, this is You. You're closing these doors. If I were to go forward, it would be complete foolishness. You are showing me it wasn't just the house; it's the area. I believe You are telling us not to move here. I don't understand why, but I am not going to disregard what Your Spirit is saying." So we dropped the idea of buying a house there and committed to revisit it again the next year.

In the meantime, my oldest daughter had a dream in which she saw us moving to a particular area about twenty minutes from where we had been living. I felt strongly that the Lord was speaking to us and to my daughter in this dream, so we went immediately and found a home in that area.

I had been prepared to buy a house more than two hours from where we had raised our children and where they were living as adults. If we had done that, we would have been separated from our children, and that distance of two hours would have dramatically changed our relationships. I had been proceeding with my own idea, but God was working behind the scenes to keep me from making a bad decision. He led us to a home just fifteen minutes from where our daughters lived.

When what had happened became clear to me, I almost wept with gratitude to the Holy Spirit.

But consider what it was like to walk through that process. I didn't know for certain that it was Messiah Jesus closing the door on that first house. I didn't know it was Him closing the door on the second house. It was His "left hand under my head," to paraphrase the maiden. I couldn't see it, but it was upholding me and guiding my decision-making. It was important to Yeshua that we remain physically close to our daughters. What a beautiful thing it is to be led by a Bridegroom who protects us, guides us, and orchestrates our circumstances, even when we don't know He's the one doing it! All I can say is, "Thank You, my Messiah, my beautiful Bridegroom, for having Your left hand under my head."

Song 2:6 ends with the bride saying, "And [let] his right hand embrace me." As I referred to earlier, the right hand speaks of the visible manifestation of the Lord's love in our lives, the things we are aware of Him doing. The embrace of God's right hand means all the things Jesus does for us that we can see—the favor He shows us, the open doors we are aware He orchestrated. We need both the right and left hand of God in our lives. If His activity were entirely invisible, our faith might wane. On the other hand, if everything He did were known to us, we wouldn't develop the strength to walk by faith and not by sight.

Let me close this chapter by praying for you.

Father God, we bless You right now, and we thank You that Your banner over us is love. Forgive us for being deceived when we see terror all around in the valleys of life. Your Word tells us in Psalm 91 that a thousand may fall at our side, and ten thousand at our right hand, but no evil will befall us or come near our dwelling, because You are our God. Help us not to fear the darkness around us. Help us to trust You and to know You are in control.

You told us in Your Word that not a sparrow falls to the ground apart from Your knowing. We ask You to release new levels of trust in You, that we would believe that the banner over our lives is love. That Your banner would take away all our fear—fear of the future, fear of losing our jobs, fear of old age, fear of running out of money, fear of health concerns, fear of what might happen in our children's lives, and on and on. We declare that whom the Son sets free is free indeed.

King Jesus, Your love is unconquerable, and we dwell under Your victorious banner. Nothing can separate us from Your love. Your Word says perfect love casts out all fear. So, Father, cast out all fear from our lives even now, through Your perfect love. Let the banner of Your powerful love reign through Your Son over our lives.

Lord Jesus, we also ask You to sustain Your people with raisin cakes. I pray especially for those who are really weak right now, who have no more power in and of themselves. Please, Messiah Jesus, come to them. Release angels to strengthen Your people. As You did with the man in my congregation by literally sending him raisin cakes, I ask You to release raisin cakes in whatever form to those who are weak in power. Sustain our faith and encourage us. Refresh us with apples because we are lovesick.

Messiah Jesus, demonstrate to us supernaturally, dynamically, and prophetically through Your Holy Spirit in a multiplicity of ways that Your presence surrounds us. Ignite our emotions so we feel what You feel. Cause us to feel beautiful in Your beauty. Cause us to feel lovely. Cause our whole lives to be filled with Your presence and fragrance, and let us carry that manifest presence with us wherever we go. We pray this in Your name and for Your fame, Messiah Jesus, Amen!

Chapter 8

COME ALONG!

THE SHULAMITE BRIDE, this prophetic picture of the church, now reaches the defining crisis in her walk with God. With no real warning, Yeshua reveals Himself to her in a challenging way that even we as readers may find surprising.

> Listen! My beloved! Behold, he is coming, climbing on the mountains, leaping on the hills!
>
> —SONG 2:8

Suddenly, she sees Yeshua climbing and jumping on mountaintops. This is her Beloved in a brand-new dimension, leaping victoriously from peak to peak. She exclaims: "My beloved is like a gazelle or a young stag" (Song 2:9).

Then suddenly He is at her place of residence, standing outside and calling for her to follow Him.

> Behold, he is standing behind our wall, he is looking through the windows, he is peering through the lattice. My beloved responded and said to me, "Arise, my darling, my beautiful one, and come along."
>
> —Song 2:9–10

Not only is He revealing himself in an unfamiliar form in an unfamiliar place, but He is beckoning her to come with Him. Twice in this passage (see also verse 13) He uses the command, "Arise." This means, "Stand up and get ready to change where you are and what you are doing. Make the first move to follow Me." All of it must have astonished, scared, and perplexed the young maiden.

Her first thought is, "No!" She doesn't like the idea of climbing a mountain. It is uncomfortable and seems dangerous and perhaps far beyond her perceived abilities. Climbing and leaping take a lot of effort. It requires leaving behind the comforts of home, and for these reasons she resists. But this initiates a problem: remaining in His presence is contingent upon following Him wherever He goes, and now the stage is set for the great internal struggle that will lead to her culminating maturity.

A Change of Season

Anyone who has walked with the Lord for some time can tell you there are different seasons of the Holy Spirit's operation in our lives. Up to now we have seen the bride bask in Messiah Jesus' fragrance and affirmation. She praised Him as better than any worldly pleasure; she described His refreshing presence as akin to raisin cakes and apples. She sat at the King's banqueting table, and her heart opened up to Him in the midst of His extravagant love and provision. She was experiencing the beginning of the journey of divine romance, like many of us did in our early days of following the Lord.

Do you remember when you first met Him, how God did so many little things for you? It was like that for me. In those early days Father God worked in so many supernatural ways. It seemed He often showed up in my circumstances and made Himself known and experienced. I loved it. He let me know He was present and active with me in so many ways, big and small. But as time went on, some of those noticeable moments stopped happening with the same frequency. As a result, I wondered what was going on. I became almost bitter because it seemed like the supernatural had stopped.

Then I understood. Yeshua was revealing to me: "You have been at this place of relative comfort, experiencing My presence and glory, for long enough. It is time for us to move on together. I'm going to ask you to step out in faith. I want you to face some things that will make you afraid. I want you to conquer some issues in your life and do new things for Me. Some of the assignments I have for you will feel uncomfortable and even strike fear into your heart for a while. But I am still asking you, *My beloved one*, to follow Me to the top of the mountain." Now it wasn't enough to declare that His trustworthy banner over my life was love—I had to move forward and walk it out by faith.

So the bride finds herself in a great dilemma: Should she stay in the familiar place she had been or enter the unknown with Him? The King encourages her that it is time for a change: "For behold, the winter is past..." (Song 2:11). In essence, He is saying, "I took you through the cold, harsh season of winter.

I have been faithful to you in all things, and now that former season is gone. You can trust Me for the future and the new things I have for us together in higher places. My banner over you is love."

He continues:

> The rain is over and gone. The flowers have already appeared in the land; the time has arrived for pruning the vines.
>
> —Song 2:11–12

We might read this and think, "Why doesn't she go with Him? Isn't this exactly what she asked for earlier—to run with Him?" But now she realizes she is being held back by areas of doubt and fear she didn't know were there. Yeshua's invitation disturbs her mind. It interrupts her peaceful repose under the apple tree where His beauty and care refreshed her. She didn't realize her own heart and mind would rebel at His command, and she has a choice to make. Will she stay in the place of comfort and refreshment, or will she overcome these internal weaknesses and go with Him to the mountaintop to partner with Him in greater ways?

My Journey Up the Mountain

When I met the Lord, I was so excited. I started telling everybody about Him. Fellow believers advised me to get a New Testament, and I devoured it with great joy, discovering who God is and my own identity in Him as His child. I started going to churches all over the city. I was so hungry for God I wanted to be in church meetings and Bible studies as much as I could. At the same time, I was still untrained in living a

Christian lifestyle. I had come right out of the world, where I used to do many unsanctified things.

One of them strikes me as comical all these years later. I would take a girl on a date to a Christian coffeehouse to listen to Christian music. But on the way, I would stop at a convenience store, pick up a six-pack of beer, and drink it in my car in the parking lot of the coffeehouse before going inside! I didn't think anything of it. (Personally, I don't believe it's sinful to drink alcohol in moderation, but I was clueless as to what might be considered normal Christian behavior.) It didn't even occur to me that it might be wrong or unhelpful. Everything about walking with Jesus was something I had to learn.

The Holy Spirit was faithful to put His finger on the issues and habits in my life that kept me from closer fellowship with Him. It was as if He said, "Now it's time to cleanse yourself of these things, to get a little whiter like that lily in the valley." I had been like the bride in the Song of Songs up to this point, soaking in Yeshua's love and being bathed in His presence. Then came a time—as it does for all of us—of unexpected shifts and tests that required faith and obedience.

I was learning that God requires greater and greater levels of obedience over time. The progression never ends, and this is for our transformation and glory. Of course, His way of leading us includes times of rest when we are simply strengthened in His presence, being still and receiving. But then He changes it up and calls us out from under the apple tree to take greater steps of faith up the mountain in our work and relationship with Him.

Moving on, the dynamic continues as He attempts to woo her, saying:

> O my dove, in the *clefts of the rock*, in the *secret place of the steep pathway*, let me see your form, let me hear your voice; for your voice is sweet, and your form is lovely.
> —Song 2:14, EMPHASIS ADDED

This entire interaction has a deep prophetic meaning. Notice He refers to "the clefts of the rock." This term appears in Moses' well-known encounter with God, related to us in Exodus 33:18–23:

> Then Moses said, "I pray You, show me Your glory!" And He said, "I Myself will make all My goodness pass before you, and will proclaim the name of the Lord before you; and I will be gracious to whom I will be gracious, and will show compassion on whom I will show compassion. But He said, "You cannot see My face, for no man can see Me and live!"
>
> Then the Lord said, "Behold, there is a place by Me, and you shall stand there on the rock; and it will come about, while My glory is passing by, that I will put you in the cleft of the rock and cover you with My hand until I have passed by. Then I will take My hand away and you shall see My back, but My face shall not be seen."

The cleft of the rock is the place Father God provides to allow us to experience His glory. Moses was not able to approach God and see His glory as a human being, so God said, in essence, "I will put you in the cleft of the rock, a place that will protect you." What does this mean for you and me? The cleft of the rock is a shadow of Jesus. Yeshua has become the cleft of the rock for us. In Him we are accepted and can experience the favor, love, glory, and revelation of God. The New Testament testifies that Messiah Jesus is the cleft of the rock for us. Paul writes in 1 Corinthians 10:4, "And all [the children of Israel] drank the same spiritual drink, for they were drinking from a spiritual rock which followed them; and the rock was Christ."

And notice also in Song 2:14 we come to the enigmatic phrase "the steep pathway." This is nothing less than the ascension and resurrection of Jesus. When we enter the cleft of the rock, we are baptized into Yeshua's resurrection and ascension. Messiah Jesus came as a man, died on the cross for our sins, and then arose from the grave and ascended to heaven. He paid a steep price to create that "secret place of the steep pathway" for those of us who have been baptized into Him. He has become the way, the truth, and the life—the path for us to God. We are covered by the sacrifice of His blood, so even when the path gets steep and our steps are imperfect, we remain in the cleft of the rock, living in the reality of His resurrection. The power of Jesus is literally manifested from on high in our lives through the secret place of the steep pathway.

He then says, "Let me hear your voice." We may think Yeshua will be irritated by our cries on the journey up the steep pathway in the secret place, but the reality is just the opposite. He says, "O my dove, in the clefts of the rock, in the secret place of the steep pathway, let me see your form, let me hear your voice; for your voice is sweet, and your form is lovely" (Song 2:14). Jesus wants us to call out to Him as we journey up through the difficult pathways of our lives. He tells the maiden, and you and me: "When you're struggling and having difficulty obeying Me, lift your voice to Me. You are in the cleft of the rock, covered by My grace, covered by My blood. You will always be beautiful to Me. Don't shrink back. Don't let Satan put shame on you and silence you, because there is no condemnation for you who are in Me. Lift your voice and pray to Me. I want to hear it! It's beautiful to Me."

That is His word to us now. Call out to Him in the difficult moments, in the steep places, in the narrow, dark times of life. He is ready to hear from us at all times.

> *Lord, I want to follow You wherever You go! I admit that at times I have been slow to say yes when You called me into a new, uncomfortable season. Thank You for Your patience with me, and forgive me for thinking the path is sometimes too daunting. I trust You as I follow You to the mountaintops of a new endeavor. I want to grow and progress in You. I want to see and experience Your glory in new and fresh ways. Help me to respond to Your coaxing as I make my way up the steep pathway of life. I know You love the sound of my voice as I call out to You in difficult times, so I cry out freely for Your help, guidance, and strength. I declare that You lead me perfectly wherever I need to go. Thank You for uniting Yourself to me and taking joy in every part of my journey.*

Chapter 9

CATCH THE FOXES

I N VERSE 15 of chapter 2 we see the bride in the midst of her hesitations. She senses that her heart is unwilling to go, yet she knows she should go with the Bridegroom to the mountaintop, so she cries out as any of us might when caught in this internal struggle. The love song puts it this way:

> Catch the foxes for us, the little foxes that are ruining the vineyards.
>
> —SONG 2:15

In other words, she cries, "Jesus, I have many little fears and insecurities. The thoughts running through my mind are making me afraid. I need help! I can't do it alone. The foxes are too crafty, too quick, and too evasive for me to control. Catch them for us, these creatures that are ruining the vineyards. I want to move forward in You, but they are hindering me!"

Are there things robbing you of your relationship with God—"little foxes," little sins, little habits, little wrong beliefs that seem to get in the way? You can call out to Messiah about them. What a relief to realize we don't have to overcome sins and obstacles by ourselves. The Shulamite bride called out to the Lord, "Help me with these insecurities, these fears, these habits, this anxiousness. Help me with these thoughts of lust, greed, selfishness, and anger." We must call out to Yeshua in the steep pathway because there is mercy for us in Him. Hallelujah!

She then acknowledges that her relationship with God is indeed growing, even during this struggle, by saying, "…while our vineyards are in blossom" (Song 2:15). What a great statement of faith right in the middle of a very tough season! She still feels alive in God, even though Satan and the forces of darkness are trying to get her to pull back from Jesus. Talk about internal tension! But somehow she digs down deep and declares the foundational, crowning reality of her life with a flash of confidence:

> My beloved is mine, and I am his.
>
> —SONG 2:16

This perspective makes all the difference for her—and for us. When we fail, too often we criticize ourselves as being rebellious. But rebellion is a heart posture to disobey God and carry out our own desires. That is not the reality or state of sincere believers trying to ascend the steep pathway with Messiah but being hindered by the "little foxes" of fear and insecurity. The bride knew the difference. She wasn't rebellious; she just didn't think she had the power to obey. She wasn't walking away from the relationship. When times got tough, she returned to what she knew to be true and declared boldly: "He is mine, and I am His—and our relationship is growing, despite what things feel or look like!"

Still, she wasn't willing to jump in with both feet to follow Him just yet:

> Until the cool of the day when the shadows flee away, turn, my beloved, and be like a gazelle or a young stag on the mountains of Bether.
>
> —Song 2:17

I like how the King James translation puts it: "Until the day break…" This is a portrait of her expectation that at some point, day will break, flooding her with greater confidence and vision so she can successfully follow Him. She tells Him, "Until I have more light on this, until I can see things differently, until the day breaks and I can see this from Your perspective, Lord Jesus, I'm asking You to turn away and go alone. I can't follow You just yet. I'm not going to the mountains with You. You keep leaping from mountain to mountain like a gazelle—it is a magnificent thing to observe. But I'm going to stay right here under the shade tree."

This is such a crucial verse—and poignantly sad. Jesus said, "If anyone loves Me, he will keep My word; and My Father will love him, and We will come to him and make Our abode with him. He who does not love Me does not keep My words; and the word which you hear is not Mine, but the Father's who sent Me" (John 14:23–24). In other words, we obey Him because we want to be where He is and abide in Him. But when we disobey, a rupture in fellowship is created. The Hebrew word translated "Bether" means separation. So a separation takes place in the young bride's life because of her disobedience. She actually knows it is caused by her fear, yet she refuses Him, not fully prepared for what following Him to the mountaintops would mean for her.

Seeking Him in the Night

Obedience may have felt costly, but her disobedience is even more costly. When we don't obey, the Lord lifts His presence from us, not to punish or reject us but because He is jealous for us and wants the loss of His felt presence to be a catalyst for us to arise and follow Him. Now we find out just how costly the Shulamite bride's disobedience is.

> On my bed night after night I sought him whom my soul loves; I sought him but did not find him.
> —Song 3:1

Fellowship has been broken. Messiah Yeshua has gone, but He hasn't changed His mind about her. He simply is not going to allow her to experience the peace of His presence while she is leading a life of disobedience.

The maiden is grieving. The one whose fellowship she enjoyed so much is apparently gone. She found she couldn't have both her disobedience and His presence. The Lord was disciplining her gently. But hear this: Jesus starts with as little discipline as He needs to get through to us, but if we don't respond to His presence lifting, His actions become more and more severe.

We see this take place rather amazingly in Revelation 2:20–23 when a woman called Jezebel set herself up as a prophetess in the church while living an immoral lifestyle. Messiah Jesus said:

> But I have this against you, that you tolerate the woman Jezebel, who calls herself a prophetess, and she teaches and leads My bond-servants astray so that they commit acts of immorality and eat things sacrificed to idols. I gave her time to repent, and she does not want to repent of her immorality. Behold, I will throw her on a bed of sickness, and those who commit adultery with her into great tribulation, unless they repent of her deeds. And I will kill her children with pestilence, and all the churches will know that I am He who searches the minds and hearts; and I will give to each one of you according to your deeds.

That's advanced discipline! He gave Jezebel time to repent. He was patient with her, but she did not yield to gentle chastening, so He warned her of less-gentle correction to come. Beloved one, if we don't yield to the Lord in the areas of life where He is dealing with us to yield to Him, a stricter form of discipline will arrive. God loves us too much to leave us where we are.

Consider your own life right now. Is there a specific area the Holy Spirit has been putting His finger on, and you know you are in disobedience but you still resist doing the right thing? If He calls you to surrender your finances to Him, release your finances to Him! If there are relationships the Lord wants you to reconsider or release, now is the time! If there are addictions or habits the Lord is calling you to forsake, do it immediately! Don't remain out of fellowship in the place of comfort and familiarity. The mountaintop awaits you—or so does greater discipline.

The bride, grieving the loss of immediate fellowship with her Beloved, now responds in a way that worked in the past but will not work now. What does she do? She prays.

> On my bed night after night I sought him.
>
> —Song 3:1

This is a picture of seeking after God. Don't get me wrong; praying is so critical. We must pray in everything we do, but there are times when prayer alone is not enough. We must also take action. Let's say someone struggles with food addictions. Prayer alone will not solve the problem. That person must decide to eat healthier and put boundaries on his consumption. Lying in bed praying about it is a start, but if you lie in your bed and never do anything to change, you won't make progress in any area of life. Eventually you will experience greater discipline from the Lord because you are not doing what God requires of you, and He is unwilling to give up on His relationship with you. As followers of Yeshua, we will never come to a place where no more change is required. We are continually being transformed. God is always calling us to a deeper level with Him, and it will always involve some form of action on our parts.

Notice that this season in the bride's life didn't last just a moment. She says she did this "night after night," meaning for an extended period. There will be seasons in our lives that last some length of time, when God is calling us to do something and we resist Him until we can't stand it anymore. Maybe we don't even realize we are in this season for a while. These are times when God is doing a work of grace and strengthening us beneath the surface, training us to walk by faith and not by feelings. Sometimes God will teach us to be obedient and faithful when we don't know exactly why we feel out of fellowship with Him.

When we understand that Father is disciplining us to mature us in Him, we may wish He would give us all the discipline we need immediately so we can move quickly through that season into a state of feeling good and blessed. But "instant discipline" is not always His way. God is not in the business of microwaving people into obedience. He takes His time because He wants true, lasting change in our hearts. Transformation takes time. We have to see that the old ways of doing things don't work anymore.

You may be going through a season of discipline in your life right now, and it seems to be lasting a while. Hebrews 12:12–13 says, "Therefore, strengthen the hands that are weak and the knees that are feeble, and make straight paths for your feet, so that the limb which is lame may not be put out of joint, but rather be healed."

Earlier in the same chapter, the writer of Hebrews exhorts us,

> And you have forgotten the exhortation which is addressed to you as sons, "My son, do not regard lightly the discipline of the Lord, nor faint when you are reproved by Him; for those whom the Lord loves He disciplines, and He scourges every son whom He receives." It is for discipline that you endure; God deals with you as with sons; for what son is there whom his father does

not discipline? But if you are without discipline, of which all have become partakers, then you are illegitimate children and not sons.

Furthermore, we had earthly fathers to discipline us, and we respected them; shall we not much rather be subject to the Father of spirits, and live? For they disciplined us for a short time as seemed best to them, but He disciplines us for our good, so that we may share His holiness. All discipline for the moment seems not to be joyful, but sorrowful; yet to those who have been trained by it, afterwards it yields the peaceful fruit of righteousness.

—Hebrews 12:5–11

If you are going through a season where you don't seem to feel the presence of God, be assured that He is still with you. He has not left you. The reason He is not manifesting Himself to you in the same way He used to may be because He wants to train you to live by faith and not by feelings. He is prying you away from the old and calling you to something new. It may require doing something more than seeking Him "night after night." It will demand of you radical obedience to go with Him to the top of a mountain, to accomplish the new, great work of transformation He is working within you.

We should welcome the Lord's discipline because it helps us to choose to go to new places and do new things that we wouldn't have chosen to do without His loving hand disciplining us. I encourage you to even ask Father God for His discipline. Jesus said in Revelation 3:19, "Those whom I love, I reprove and discipline." So join me in praying for this!

Father, I come on behalf of myself and those reading these words. We are so thankful that You love us and call us Your children. You told us in Your Word that even as a father disciplines the son in whom he delights, so You discipline us because You delight in us. We thank You for Your discipline because we want to walk with You in the high places of blessing.

We are counting on Your discipline to shepherd us to the mountaintop. We ask for Your discipline. We want You to accomplish everything You envision in our lives. We don't want to get away with doing anything less. Your Word says the end result of discipline is the peaceful fruit of righteousness, and we invite that process and that result into our lives.

Yeshua, I pray for those who are in a season of Bether (separation) in their lives: for those who can't feel Your presence because of disobedience in their lives; for some who are right now reading this and know that there are things You have put Your finger on in their lives for which they are unwilling to repent of; for those precious ones of Yours who have been unwilling to follow You up the mountain and are like the maiden lying in bed alone, praying but not feeling You. For these, I pray, Father. Thank You that You are not finished with any of us yet! I ask You to touch us and give us the abundant grace needed to move on.

Thank You for putting us in the cleft of the rock, the place where You tenderly nurture us. Thank You for ascending to heaven that we could enter in to the steep pathway and the secret place as partakers of Your resurrection power. Now strengthen us in our weakness and cause us to become more than conquerors through You. We ask you to catch all the little foxes in our lives that impair the blossoming of Your love and purpose in us.

Thank You that we don't have to do it alone. We call upon You to extinguish the little insecurities, fears, selfishness, vain ambitions, and other areas of sin that hinder us from running. We give You glory for it and thank You that Your victory is secure and Your banner of unconquerable love is over us!

Chapter 10

I HAVE FOUND HIM WHOM
MY SOUL LOVES

A FTER A SEASON of discipline, the Shulamite bride real-izes she is not going to find her Beloved just by lying in her bed praying. She now declares:

> I must arise now and go about the city; in the streets and in the squares I must seek him whom my soul loves.
>
> —SONG 3:2

For the first time she echoes His command to "arise." There's just one problem: her obedience is incomplete. Instead of arising to go to the top of the mountain where He called her to, she arises and goes about the city. It is almost as if she is bargaining with her Beloved, offering to obey in part but not the whole.

I wonder how many times you and I are like that. God asks

us to do something specific, and we try to compromise with Him and say, "OK, Lord, I'll do it this way but not that way." How many times do we spur ourselves to action—but not the action He wants? Rather, we go to the place of distractions, which is represented in this verse by "the city."

The city is not necessarily a bad or sinful place, but in this situation she goes to the city in disobedience to God's command. Think of it like this: maybe the Lord is calling someone to serve in a homeless shelter, but instead of obeying, he increases his Christian activity by going to all sorts of conferences, reading numerous books by Christian authors, and joining Bible studies—all while avoiding being obedient to serve at the homeless shelter to which he has been called.

Beloved ones, we will not find the Lord unless we obey Him! The deep fellowship we desire does not come without obedience. God will not be impressed if we are running diligently around "the city" when He has called us to "the mountaintop."

Next she tries another form of avoidance.

> The watchmen who make the rounds in the city found me, and I said, "Have you seen him whom my soul loves?"
> —SONG 3:3

Now instead of going to the mountaintop, she goes to the spiritual authorities in the city, but they are not equipped to answer her in her current, self-created plight. Many pastors know the experience of having someone come and ask them for counsel on a particular matter, and the pastor simply has no answer to give because the person is avoiding something the Lord told him or her to do. They are like the bride, seeking answers in a place that is familiar but does not hold the key of release and peace they are looking for.

Some kind of intervention is needed to arrest the maiden's attention and get her back on the right path. So there in her disobedience Jesus reveals Himself to her anew to draw her beyond that place.

> Scarcely had I left them when I found him whom my soul loves; I held on to him and would not let him go until I had brought him to my mother's house, and into the room of her who conceived me.
>
> —SONG 3:4

Jesus had never left her, but He had withdrawn His presence. He was disciplining her. His reappearance here after the season of discipline inspires greater determination in her than ever before, and she says, "This time I'm never going to let Him go!" In other words, "I'm not going to let disobedience get in the way of my relationship with my Bridegroom, King Jesus, ever again!"

Seize My Word, and Don't Let Anything Else In

Years ago the Lord spoke audibly to me in a dream. I heard the voice of the Lord, and it was so powerful. Not only did I hear the Lord's voice, but I literally felt the motion of the Holy Spirit—the power and fire of His love—rolling into my soul and back to Himself. That's the only way I know to describe it. Then the Holy Spirit spoke these words to my ears: "Seize My Word, and don't let anything else in." I take this command seriously and am earnestly striving to live it out.

That experience reminds me of what the Shulamite bride says here. Upon seeing Him up close again, she exhibits a fierce determination that can only be produced by the Holy Spirit. It's as if she is saying, "I am seizing You, and I won't let anything else in!"

My Mother's Room

Continuing, she says, "I…brought him to my mother's house, and into the room of her who conceived me" (Song 3:4). What could this phrase mean for you and me?

The phrase "the room of her who conceived me" indicates that we should bring Jesus into the deepest and most private areas of our beings. To her credit, the bride says, "I'm going to give You access to all of me. I want You to have Your way in every place in my life. You are not trespassing. I was created by You and for You. I don't belong to myself anymore."

Consider also that she brought Him into her home environment. Does your relationship with Yeshua permeate every room in your house and all the relationships that are being lived out inside it?

Leave a Tender Season Alone

Then the Bridegroom says, "I adjure you, O daughters of Jerusalem," meaning believers who aren't as spiritually sensitive and mature, "by the gazelles or by the hinds of the field, that you will not arouse or awaken my love until she pleases" (Song 3:5).

The Lord is saying that this season is sacred; don't let anybody disturb it. Gazelles are sensitive animals and easily spooked. When you see a deer in nature, and it sees you, it usually bounds off into the woods. Sometimes we are the same way. There are seasons in our lives and in the lives of others when God is doing such a deep work that we need to give it space and not allow anything to disrupt it. The Holy Spirit here warns the friends of the bride not to disturb His deep work in her life.

Years ago I went through a season in which the Lord was doing something so beautiful in my heart. To make room for what He was doing, I disconnected from as many responsibilities as I could. I just wanted to be able to sit before the Lord, even as Mary sat at Jesus' feet, to allow Him to work fully in me. But I had some "daughters of Jerusalem" in my life who couldn't understand what was going on. I tried to explain to them that the Holy Spirit was doing a deep work within me, and that was why I was setting aside some responsibilities for a season, but they couldn't understand it.

They started making excuses for me to others, saying, "Oh, he's just going through something. It'll pass. Everybody goes through things." They made it sound negative, as if I was burdened with some heavy load. Not at all! There are seasons in life when the Holy Spirit ministers to us and brings us to a new level in the Lord Jesus. We need to be careful when these seasons are happening not to disrupt what He is doing by getting too busy or by letting personal interactions disturb us.

We also must do the same when we sense that somebody else is being deeply impacted by the Holy Spirit. Be careful not to disrupt what is happening. Let's not be like the daughters of Jerusalem who needed more sensitivity. Don't pry, don't keep asking questions, and don't demand explanations. Give them plenty of space "until love pleases," and allow the Spirit to finish His job undisturbed.

Up From the Wilderness

As the bride says yes to the Bridegroom in her still-limited way, He begins to bring her through the wilderness. The wildernesses represent those things in life that must be overcome. Messiah Jesus overcame the devil in the wilderness (Matthew 4). The wilderness can also represent a time of feeling lost or empty. Maybe you feel you are in a wilderness right now. If so, Yeshua identifies with you and knows how to get you through that wilderness. He never fails, and that is why the Shulamite bride now sees Him coming up out of the wilderness victorious and glorious.

> What is this coming up from the wilderness like columns of smoke, perfumed with myrrh and frankincense, with all scented powders of the merchant?
> —Song 3:6

We might reasonably ask, "What is Jesus doing in the wilderness?" It is true that He never wandered away from the Father, but He had to defeat Satan in the wilderness and was identifying with you and me in our sinfulness, brokenness, and weakness. He was neither sinful nor weak but made Himself totally vulnerable to the human plight and overcame all on our behalf.

Messiah comes up victorious from the wilderness, uniting Himself with us in our journey through our own personal wildernesses. He demonstrates His complete identification with us and His power to overcome things we cannot. The bride sees Him come up out of the wilderness with columns of smoke, representing the glory of God, and all the scented powders of the merchant, which speak of His value as the most beautiful and precious One in all creation.

And He is traveling up through the wilderness on a bridal couch (Song 3:7–11). The picture is, quite profoundly, one of you and me. We pass through wildernesses of suffering, learning, disobedience, transformation, and correction, but our destiny to be His bride is always certain. We overcome with Him as the Holy Spirit carries us through the wilderness toward the marriage supper of the Lamb.

She describes the glory of this in beautiful military and tabernacle language.

> Sixty mighty men around it, of the mighty men of Israel.
> All of them are wielders of the sword, expert in war
> —Song 3:7–8

This tells us we are protected on this journey through the wilderness, and those guarding us are more than mercenaries. The sixty around the bridal couch are some of the mighty men of Israel. In the ancient world, sometimes men would join an army because they were paid to do so. They didn't have any particular interest in the objective of the army in which they enlisted. They simply did it as a profession. That is not the case with God's kingdom. The ones guarding our lives are committed to their King and to us, His bride. They live for the cause of protecting us.

The Song continues by telling us, "Each man has his sword at his side, guarding against the terrors of the night" (Song 3:8). This speaks to the complete readiness of God's angels that are protecting us. Nothing catches them by surprise. Angels surround you. You are the apple of Father God's eye. Not a sparrow falls to the ground without Him knowing it. We are safe. David sang it this way:

> The LORD is my light and my salvation; whom shall I fear? The LORD is the defense of my life; whom shall I dread? When evildoers came upon me to devour my flesh, my adversaries and my enemies, they stumbled and fell. Though a host encamp against me, my heart will not fear; though war arise against me, in spite of this I shall be confident.
>
> —PSALM 27:1–3

The Lord wants to build a sense of security into our lives. He wants us to deeply receive into our souls the revelation that we are well-protected on this earth. I don't know about you, but I pray all the time that the Lord will make me secure. When I look around, I see a world where evil abounds and bad things seem to happen at random—catastrophes, car wrecks, people losing jobs, losing their houses, losing their health. I know that if not for the protection of God in my life, random evil and chaos would destroy me. So I cry out to God, "Help me to know that You are protecting me. Help me to know that I am secure." This passage in the Song is one way He assures us that we are safe.

The word *sixty* in verse 7 ("Sixty mighty men around it, of the mighty men of Israel") reflects tabernacle language. There were sixty poles or sixty pillars that held up the tabernacle in the wilderness. The tabernacle was the place where God dwelled with man, as is revealed in the Hebrew Bible

(Exod. 25:8). Military and tabernacle language flow beautifully together here, combining the realities of protection and the abiding presence of God in our lives. As David sang in the midst of the siege described in the psalm previously quoted:

> One thing I have asked from the LORD, that I shall seek: that I may dwell in the house of the Lord all the days of my life, to behold the beauty of the LORD and to meditate in His temple. For in the day of trouble He will conceal me in His tabernacle; in the secret place of His tent He will hide me; He will lift me up on a rock. And now my head will be lifted up above my enemies around me, and I will offer in His tent sacrifices with shouts of joy; I will sing, yes, I will sing praises to the LORD.
>
> —PSALM 27:4–6

The Best in the World

We might think a caravan and a couch coming up from the wilderness would look dusty, beat-up, and ragged. But not this one!

> King Solomon has made for himself a sedan chair from the timber of Lebanon. He made its posts of silver, its back of gold and its seat of purple fabric, with its interior lovingly fitted out by the daughters of Jerusalem.
>
> —SONG 3:9–10

As with any description of heavenly things, words never do it justice. The bride does her best, describing the King's wedding couch/chair in terms of the finest materials known to man at that time. The timber of Lebanon, for example, was the most costly and fragrant timber one could buy. The couch's posts were made of silver, speaking of redemption; its back of gold, speaking of the character of God; its seat of purple fabric, speaking of royalty and authority. And its interior was "paved with love," as the King James Version puts it in verse 10.

This language builds anticipation in our hearts leading up to the royal wedding processional and prophetically to the marriage supper of the Lamb. We are the ones riding on this bridal couch with Jesus, which is made of the most preeminent, supernatural, spiritual substances!

The Holy Spirit then instructs us in verse 11: "Go forth, O daughters of Zion, and gaze on King Solomon with the crown with which his mother has crowned him on the day of his wedding, and on the day of his gladness of heart." The Holy Spirit is saying, "Look at King Jesus and gaze upon His glory! Behold your Bridegroom God. He is coming for you. Get a glimpse of His love."

Notice again that the King's mother has crowned Him (Song 3:7). In the Gospels, Jesus said that the church—made up of His followers—is His "mother."

> And stretching out His hand toward His disciples, He said, "Behold My mother and My brothers!"
> —MATTHEW 12:49

We, His followers, are the ones privileged to crown Him with the gift of our love. Nobody can crown Him with that gift but you.

As we close this chapter, let's review. The bride finally arises but stays within the zone of her present comfort, seeking answers in familiar places and in known ways. Although the bride had not reached a state of full maturity or absolute obedience, the King surprises her by appearing to her where she is. She then clutches Him, declaring that this time she will never let Him go. Not only that, but she brings Him into the deepest places of her own heart.

As a result of her renewed commitment, the Holy Spirit warns everyone involved to respect and not disrupt this sensitive season the bride is now experiencing. Next, the bride, who is a shadow of you and me, sees her King coming up from the wilderness on a bridal couch in which she too travels. This couch is superior in every way, from its construction materials to its colors, from its textures to its scents. It symbolizes the excellency of journeying with Messiah Jesus through life as we travel through many wildernesses on our way to the marriage supper of the Lamb. Traveling with the King and the church are elite warriors, protecting us from any malevolent influence. Lastly, the Shulamite bride responds to all this by crowning King Jesus with the affections of her heart.

I invite you to respond to this magnificent picture of your life and future with Yeshua in the same way:

> *King Jesus, I love You today! I crown You with the crown of my affections. I honor and extol You. I am so looking forward to the marriage supper of the Lamb. I ask You to remove every hindrance to my love. Whatever is standing in the way of You having Your full way in my life, remove it. Set me ablaze with love for You. Produce within me a holy violence to seize You by the Holy Spirit, to resolve with all my heart, strength, soul, and mind to not let You go. I come to You realizing I cannot produce this fierce spiritual determination by my own efforts. Thank*

You for journeying with me through the wildernesses and for being completely victorious. Thank You for the excellence of all Your works. And thank You for guarding me from danger with Your holy angels and loyal love.

Chapter 11

THE BEAUTY OF THE BRIDE

OUR BRIDEGROOM GOD is quick to affirm us when we move in the right direction, and the Shulamite bride experiences that now. She has "arisen" and pledged her willingness to obey. Notice she hasn't gone to the top of the mountain yet. The only thing that has changed is her willingness to go. But as soon as she says yes in her heart, Yeshua affirms her in His love.

> How beautiful you are, my darling, how beautiful you are!
>
> —SONG 4:1

Some people think the primary way God grows us in Him is by condemning us, but that is not true. The primary way God brings us into maturity is by cherishing us! I'm grateful for the Lord's discipline, but I'm forever thankful that the main way He brings my character and will into line with His is by lavishly loving me.

A dream I had some years back touched me so much. In this dream I was being disciplined by a father figure. It wasn't my natural father. It was a symbolic, prophetic representative of a father. He was an older man and was disciplining me as a son, but the way he disciplined me was so gentle and tender. That was the entire dream, and it reminded me of what David said in Psalm 18:35, speaking to the Lord: "Your gentleness makes me great." I love that. God disciplined David, but the primary feeling David had was of the goodness, the gentleness, the tenderness of God. Those are what produce change in our lives.

Again, Jesus affirmed Peter and called him "the rock," even though He knew Peter would deny Him very soon. Peter was about to fail Him massively, and yet Jesus defined Peter by his best characteristics, not his biggest blunders. Even in your worst moments, you are a child of God whom Jesus purchased with His own blood. Your identity has been settled in heaven and on earth forever. Hallelujah! Messiah Jesus treats you as He did Peter, by calling out the budding virtues in your life. He knows we aren't done "cooking" yet. Nobody is where we need to be. Yeshua looks ahead to our fullest potential and interacts with us now based on that reality. It gives Him great joy to teach us that way.

More Doves

Once the bride expresses a willing heart, He praises her from the top of her head to the soles of her feet. He begins by saying,

Your eyes are like doves' eyes behind your veil.

—Song 4:1

Eyes are the window to the soul. You can see inside a person, so to speak, through their eyes. Eyes tell us if a person has been crying or laughing, or if they are in love or grieving or just content. Earlier I said that doves are faithful and loyal, lacking peripheral vision and mating once for life. But there is something else the Bible tells us about doves. Consider that when Jesus came out of the Jordan River after His baptism, John the Baptist saw the Holy Spirit descend from heaven upon Yeshua in the form of a dove.

There must be something to the fact that the Holy Spirit chose a dove to represent His form. I see it this way: when Jesus speaks of His church and children having doves' eyes, perhaps He means we have the same supernatural anointing upon us that manifested upon Him as a dove at His baptism in the Jordan River. Born-again people do not live solely in the natural realm anymore. We possess eternal life. There is a supernatural aspect to our lives now that we should recognize and celebrate.

Jesus looks at you and me and sees the supernatural life in us. He sees His own life in us. He sees His power in us, the same power that raised Him from the dead. There is something more than the earthly about us. We have doves' eyes because we are walking in the life and power of the Holy Spirit.

A Becoming Modesty

The veil mentioned here in chapter 4, verse 1 speaks of modesty. Jesus sees His church as elegant and becoming. Have you noticed that some people possess no modesty? They speak and act obnoxiously and put themselves out there all the time in a crass or vulgar way. They clearly lack confident security in God. They might bluff that they have all the confidence in the world, but they are actually overcompensating for the confidence they lack.

People who are confident deep down display modesty. I'm not saying confident people don't have outgoing personalities but that people who know Jesus have the confidence to be self-contained and are hidden in the Holy Spirit by the supernatural veil of true peace. They know who they are in Him.

The Meaning of "Hair"

The Bridegroom goes on to say, "Your hair is like a flock of goats" (Song 4:1). That's strange language for us to understand. What woman wants her hairstylist to tell her she has hair like a flock of goats? Not good for repeat business! But the Song of Songs was written in an agricultural time and in "earthy" language. They didn't have all the modern technology and gadgets we do. They had natural tools and techniques, so speaking of hair as thick and full as goats' hair was actually a high compliment.

But let's go beneath the surface and ask, What does hair speak of in Scripture? One of the more prominent passages about it is in Numbers 6, which talks about the Nazarite vow. When a man wanted to completely dedicate himself to God, one thing he did was shave off all his hair, then let it grow without cutting it again. Hair, then, is a symbol of dedication.

We also read about hair in 1 Corinthians 11:6, where it is a symbol of being in submission to divine authority. So when the King praises the Shulamite's (and our) hair, He is praising the beauty of her dedication to Him. He is honoring her for living under His authority.

The Power of "Teeth"

> Your teeth are like a flock of newly shorn ewes which have come up from their washing, all of which bear twins.
>
> —SONG 4:2

The bride's teeth were white and clean, not in an artificial and cosmetic way but naturally so, like newly washed sheep. What does this mean? He is talking about the words that proceed from our mouths. The Bible says we should speak words that are healthy and pure, words that encourage and build up others and ourselves, words that conform to God's Spirit and Word. But sometimes we let bitter words come from between our teeth, and we speak unnecessary criticisms and words of frustration. The Bible says that from the same faucet should not come both clear water and polluted water. Jesus wants us to get victory over this battle and have "clean teeth," so to speak.

There is something divine about the mouth. It is one of the attributes that make us like God. We are created in the image of God with the ability to communicate deeply and clearly. God spoke, and creation came into existence. We also create spiritual and physical realities by what we speak. Words are creative agents of God. They have spiritual substance. Words are the expression of thoughts, which are spiritual.

If we speak words of cursing and foulness, our whole disposition is shrouded in darkness. When we speak words of life, we feel so much better than when we find ourselves complaining and criticizing. It is pretty easy to sense when we are talking in a way that pleases the Spirit—or not. Clean talk lifts the heart and gives a sense of approval and favor. Negative or unclean talk gives a feeling of death and darkness. When gossiping about people, criticizing, complaining, worrying, fearing, or cursing like the world does, we can readily sense that those things grieve the Holy Spirit. The words of our mouths direct us and others into either life or death.

James says that if we can control the words that come from our mouths, we will determine the destinies of our lives (James 3). So the Bridegroom (Jesus) praises the bride's teeth because He hears her speaking words of life. The Bible says we overcome by the blood of the Lamb and the word of our testimony (Rev. 12:11). Words are important! We even use our mouths to confess salvation, as Romans 10:10 says: "If you confess with your mouth Jesus as Lord, and believe in your heart that God raised Him from the dead, you will be saved; for with the heart a person believes, resulting in righteousness, and with the mouth he confesses, resulting in salvation."

Jesus expects His bride to speak words of life. As you and I discipline ourselves to do this and not curse or speak words of fear and death, we will walk in a greater fruitfulness. Verse 2 of chapter 4 goes on to say, "...all of which bear twins, and not one among them has lost her young." All the sheep were fruitful. This presents a picture of abundance. When our words line up with God's Word and we bring them into agreement with the Holy Spirit, we can expect an exponential increase of abundance. Jesus said in John 15:5, "He who abides in Me and I in him, he bears much fruit, for apart from Me you can do nothing." He promises the Shulamite bride that because her teeth speak words of life, there will be a double portion of the Lord's anointing and blessing on her life.

One of the primary ways we abide in Yeshua is by speaking His words, that is, things that are pleasing to Him. Jesus said:

> For the mouth speaks out of that which fills the heart. The good man brings out of his good treasure what is good; and the evil man brings out of his evil treasure what is evil. But I tell you that every careless word that people speak, they shall give an accounting for it in the day of judgment. For by your words you will be justified, and by your words you will be condemned.
>
> —MATTHEW 12:34 37

He also said, "Truly I say to you, *whoever says* to this mountain, 'Be taken up and cast into the sea,' and does not doubt in his heart, but believes that what he says is going to happen, it will be *granted* him" (Mark 11:23, emphasis added).

The Bridegroom's next statement ties in: "Your lips are like a scarlet thread, and your mouth is lovely" (Song 4:3). Lips are the gateway to physical intimacy. What do women put on their lips to make them more attractive? Often some shade of red lipstick. Where does physical intimacy often start? With kissing. So the Lord again reveals His desire for spiritual closeness with His people.

He goes on:

> Your temples are like a slice of a pomegranate behind your veil,
>
> —SONG 4:3

The Hebrew word translated "temples" can carry with it the idea of a countenance or emotions. Yeshua is conveying again that He loves how our faces show our emotions in a variety of ways. Messiah Jesus embraces our emotions.

Strong and Nurturing

The Bridegroom's description of His bride continues in the next verse:

> Your neck is like the tower of David, built with rows of stones on which are hung a thousand shields, all the round shields of the mighty men.
>
> —Song 4:4

What does this mean? What qualities does He see in her neck? The neck is a biblical symbol of the will. God often spoke of the Israelites as a stiff-necked people. In Deuteronomy 10:16, the Lord said, "So circumcise your heart, and stiffen your neck no longer." So in the Song He is saying to her, "Your neck is like David's tower—strong and regal, built for great purposes." He is also calling to mind the fact that David was a man after His own heart. A good "neck" means a will yielded to Him and a heart after His own.

He goes on:

> Your two breasts are like two fawns, twins of a gazelle which feed among the lilies.
>
> —Song 4:5

Some people's imaginations get carried away with this picture. The funniest interpretation I have heard was when a commentator said the two breasts referred to here are the Old and New Testaments. Interesting idea, but I don't believe that's what was meant. I believe Jesus is saying that a nurturing quality flows from His bride's life. She is giving and nurturing. Breasts symbolize giving. Among the Hebrew names of God, El Shaddai (God Almighty) is related to the Hebrew word *shad*, which means breast, particularly a mother's breast.[1] It carries the sense that God nourishes His people like a mother nourishing her baby.

Some people seem to do the opposite. They take life from you because they are self-centered and negative, and everything is about them. But the bride's breasts "are like two fawns, twins of a gazelle which feed among the lilies." She is a giving, selfless person. She nourishes her children. Her life becomes a source of sustenance to help people grow and mature. So should ours be. It's not about what others can do for us, and it's not only about what God can do for us. It's also about how we can bring pleasure to God. How do we bring Him pleasure? When we serve other people and lay down our lives for them as Jesus laid down His life for us, we move His heart.

A few lines later He says,

> You are altogether beautiful, my darling, and there is no blemish in you.
>
> —SONG 4:7

Thirteen times He calls her beautiful, but now He says she is "altogether beautiful," and He does this in response to her decision to finally trust Him and go all the way to the top of the mountain. Once she pledges herself without reservation to go all the way with her lover, Messiah Yeshua proclaims that she is "altogether beautiful."

Take a minute to pray this for your own life:

> *King Jesus, I thank You that You have made me worthy through Your blood. And I thank You that You are at work in my life, both to will and to do of Your good pleasure (Phil. 2:13, KJV). Thank You for appreciating every beautiful aspect in me that You have made. Help me to choose words that please You, Lord. Show me how to be a selfless, nurturing person. Ignite my heart with divine fire. Cause me to arise and go with You to the mountaintops, where You have called me to be with You.*

Chapter 12

MYRRH, LIONS, AND WINE

THE BRIDE SPEAKS now, saying:

Until the cool of the day when the shadows flee away, I will go my way to the mountain of myrrh and to the hill of frankincense.

—SONG 4:6

Here we see again the mountain He had called her to in chapter 2 that she felt she could not surmount. But now she has reversed course and declares, "I am going to the mountain and will go until the shadows flee away. I will follow You until there is no shadow of doubt about my commitment. I am going with You all the way up that mountain!"

There is much depth in her words. Notice she says in Song 4:6, "I will go my way." God has created different journeys—"ways"—for each of us to travel with Him. Every believer has unique features in their path. Peter had to learn this lesson too. When he started asking Jesus about John's future, "Jesus said to him, 'If I want him to remain until I come, what is that to you? You follow Me!'" (John 21:22). While all journeys lead to the same place—the wedding day with Jesus—the scenery up the mountain is different for each of us. We should all say as she does, "I will go my way and do what You have for me. I set my will to walk the unique path You have called me to walk."

The Mountain of Myrrh

Why is the destination called the mountain of myrrh? As we saw earlier, myrrh is a costly spice that smells good but tastes bitter. It was used as an embalming substance, so Scripture at times associates it with death. Prophetically, we can read into the Song that the bride was recognizing that going up the mountain meant the death of the fleshly. Jesus was leaping on the mountain of myrrh because He was obedient unto death, even death on a cross (Phil. 2:8). He had triumphed over it! He calls you and me up that same mountain of myrrh so we identify with Him in the fellowship of His sufferings. Simply put, obedience to God requires death to oneself.

Myrrh is also fragrant in the positive sense. Scripture says that when we obey we become a fragrant aroma to God in Christ. This beautiful fragrance is released only when we put to death the deeds of the flesh. Paul writes in Romans 8:13, "For if you are living according to the flesh, you must die; but if by the Spirit you are putting to death the deeds of the body, you will live." We must put to death the deeds of the flesh and go up the mountain of myrrh.

I tell a story in my book *Called to Breakthrough* about an

incident in my spiritual journey that took place back in 1981. I was sitting in a chair one morning while going through a season of repentance. Day by day I was turning things over to God that He was identifying in my life. That morning, totally unexpectedly, the Spirit of God visibly appeared above my head and manifested Himself in all the colors of a rainbow. I could clearly see Him with my spiritual eyes, twirling above my head, and the sight amazed, captivated, and marked me.

Then He came down through my head into my inner man, and He spoke four simple words: "I am a servant." Then it was over, just like that. My response was uncompromising: "That settles it, God. I am going all the way with You." The experience marked me in such an incredible way. I said in my heart the same thing the Shulamite bride said to King Jesus: "Until the cool of the day when the shadows flee away, I will go my way to the mountain of myrrh and to the hill of frankincense. I will not let anything hinder me. I am going to follow You!"

Dens of Lions

On the way to the top of the mountain, there are many dangers that require us to engage in spiritual warfare. And so the Bridegroom says,

> May you come with me from Lebanon. Journey down from the summit of Amana, from the summit of Senir and Hermon, *from the dens of lions*, from the mountains of leopards.
>
> —Song 4:8, emphasis added

Dens of lions and mountains of leopards represent attacks we sustain from the enemy of our souls. In fact, Satan in

Scripture is portrayed as a roaring lion that roams about looking for someone to devour (1 Pet. 5:8). The truth is we can't fully know Messiah Jesus until we have defeated the devil as He did, and we can't defeat the devil until we become aware of him. The Scriptures tell us not to be ignorant of the schemes of Satan (2 Cor. 2:11). How would you like to go to war against an enemy you knew nothing about and couldn't see? It would be impossible to win. When we are ignorant of the evil one's tactics, we empower him by our inaction. I like to discover everything I can about spiritual warfare. In bookstores I always go to the biography section so I can find autobiographies of spiritual people who have had encounters with God and are experienced in withstanding the devil's schemes.

God demands that we become aware of the spiritual conflict we are in. He wants to give us understanding into the nature of the battle so we can face our enemy. He wants to train us by His Spirit to overcome. By definition, overcomers must have something to overcome. In Revelation 2 and 3, several times Jesus refers to "he who overcomes." King David, the great friend of God, declared that the Lord trained him for battle and even taught him to bend a bow of bronze (Ps. 18:34). David was a highly skilled warrior—just like the God we serve. The Bible tells us God is a God of war (Exod. 15:3). He stirs up His mighty power and uses it to aggressively oppose darkness (Isa. 42:13). As His children we must exhibit a fierce determination in the Spirit to do the same. We must be willing to face the enemy, take authority over him, crush him, and subdue him under our feet. Yeshua said that with the authority He has given us, we are able "to tread on serpents and scorpions, and over all the power of the enemy, and nothing will injure [us]" (Luke 10:19).

A critical part of each of our callings is to pass through the "dens of lions" and "mountains of leopards." Too many Christians find this subject scary, but with Messiah Jesus there is nothing to fear. He is guaranteeing that He will lead us successfully upward and onward.

Captivating Jesus

In the next verse, Yeshua says to His church:

> You have made my heart beat faster, my sister, my bride;
> you have made my heart beat faster with a single glance
> of your eyes, with a single strand of your necklace.
> —SONG 4:9

Many of us think of Jesus as somehow too holy to share in or be moved by our human experience. But consider that John 1:14 says the Word of God "became flesh, and dwelt among us." We sometimes tend to think of Father God as distant and separate from our lived experience. We think of Him as our provider, our protector, our Creator, but we don't often imagine Him being moved or receiving pleasure from our love for Him. But the truth is our God humbly clothed Himself in humanity and identifies with us to such a degree that He feels what we feel. The Son of God gets excited over His bride's love for Him. Some translations of Song 4:9—including the King James Version, Amplified Bible, and the Modern English Version—read, "You have ravished my heart." The clear meaning is that when we put Him first in our lives, it excites Him, blesses Him, and brings Him pleasure and happiness!

God said to Israel in Isaiah 62:5, "As the bridegroom rejoices over the bride, so your God will rejoice over you." In Isaiah 65:19, He said, "I will also rejoice in Jerusalem and be glad in My people." While He is eternally complete and lacks nothing, somehow He has arranged things so that we can add to His pleasure. Some people think that if God could get joy out of our loving Him, it would somehow make Him "less than." But the opposite is true. God is so secure and complete in Himself that with no loss of any kind He can put Himself in a position to be touched by us.

The Bible says Jesus keeps track of every single act of love we perform (Matt. 10:42). Every time you get up early in the morning to spend time with Him, it moves His heart. Every time you are gracious when someone is mean to you, it means something to Him. Every time you let someone go in front of you in traffic in order to abide in Him, He delights. Every time you breathe a prayer for a loved one—or for an enemy—Jesus knows it, feels it, and rejoices in it.

Twenty-five years ago I began to lead my home in a stronger way of practicing our Jewish identity by strictly celebrating Shabbat as well as putting more emphasis on Jewish holidays. At first my children resisted it because it got in the way of other things they were accustomed to doing, but I was patient with them as I put in place new rules that felt a little burdensome to them. But every time they resisted, it hurt me. Finally, after this went on for about a year, I exploded one day, bursting into tears.

"You're hurting me!" I cried out. My kids were shocked.

They had no idea they could hurt me. To them I was their dad, the big guy who made all the rules. When they saw they had the power to hurt me, it completely opened up their hearts to me, and things radically changed.

It is much the same way with us and God. We don't imagine we have any power to bring Him joy or to hurt him. Consider the scripture that says, "Do not grieve the Holy Spirit of God" (Eph. 4:30). The word *grieve* means to create distress or cause suffering. We can make God sad. Conversely, when we choose to love Him and put Him first in our lives, it makes His heart beat faster. It adds to our Maker's happiness.

Sweetness of Speech

The Bridegroom continues,

> Your lips, my bride, drip honey; honey and milk are under your tongue.
>
> —Song 4:11

Honey takes a lot of effort to produce. Bees do amazing amounts of work to create it. When our lips speak positive things and we hold our tongues from voicing thoughts that bring death, it takes a lot of work, and our Messiah recognizes it. It is sweet to Him.

"Milk and honey" is also the Bible's way of talking about abundance. When the Lord brought the children of Israel into the Promised Land, He described it as "a land flowing with milk and honey" (Exod. 3:17). He is saying to us here, "It has taken a lot of effort for you to get to this place where you now are, and from now on you will experience greater abundance in your life."

Next He speaks about her garments: "And the fragrance of your garments is like the fragrance of Lebanon" (Song 4:10). The Hebrew word translated "Lebanon" here actually means white. He is saying her garments are white—pure and holy. Revelation 7:13–17 also speaks of the bride's garments as white. It tells us (emphasis added):

> Then one of the elders answered, saying to me, "These who are *clothed in the white robes*, who are they, and where have they come from?" I said to him, "My lord, you know." And he said to me, "These are the ones who come out of the great tribulation, and they have washed their robes and made them white in the blood of the Lamb. For this reason, they are before the throne of God; and they serve Him day and night in His temple; and He who sits on the throne will spread His tabernacle over them. They will hunger no longer, nor thirst anymore; nor will the sun beat down on them, nor any heat; for the Lamb in the center of the throne will be their shepherd, and will guide them to springs of the water of life; and God will wipe every tear from their eyes."

The Book of Revelation also says, "It was given to her to clothe herself in fine linen, bright and clean; for the fine linen is the righteous acts of the saints" (Rev. 19:8). And in Revelation 16:15, we read, "Behold, I am coming like a thief. Blessed is the one who stays awake and keeps his clothes, so that he will not walk about naked and men will not see his shame." Yeshua also advises the church at Laodicea to buy from Him white garments (Rev. 3:18).

As the Holy Spirit cleanses us, sanctifies us, and transforms us, you and I come to look more and more like Jesus. The Bible says we will one day shine like the stars forever. Romans 8:29–30 says: "For those whom He foreknew, He also predestined to become conformed to the image of His Son, so that He would be the firstborn among many brethren; and these whom He predestined, He also called; and these whom He called, He also justified; and these whom He justified, He also glorified." Beloved one, you are greater than you realize!

Not only is the bride white with purity, but she belongs entirely to Jesus. He says to her,

A garden locked is my sister, my bride, a rock garden locked, a spring sealed up.

—Song 4:12

In the ancient world there were two types of gardens: private and public. Public gardens were open for anybody to enjoy, but wealthy people often had private gardens, locked and sealed for their own enjoyment. So Yeshua says, "You are to Me as a sealed garden, exclusively for Me. Nothing will come in that defiles or pollutes. You exist for My pleasure." We must put boundaries of protection around our lives, not allowing the defiling influence of the world inside. This is why we should not watch things on television or in movies that, while they might be interesting or entertaining, pollute our souls. We don't get to reserve some of our lives for our own enjoyment. The garden belongs to Him.

For years I tried to keep the area of eating from the Holy Spirit's control. God desires us to have pleasure in food. After all, He equipped us with taste buds. But this pleasure must be under His authority. I didn't want to hand over my eating of pastries, cookies, and candy to Messiah. I had to cut back on unhealthy foods if I was to become a "locked garden" to Him by respecting my body, the temple of His Spirit. If we are suffering from obesity, high blood pressure, or other physical problems resulting from an untamed appetite, we have to face the reality that we are disrespecting and defiling where God lives. Lack of health never feels good, and it limits what we are able to do for and with God. Keep your body as if God lives in it—because He does! It is part of His "garden locked."

Orchards of Abundance

Yeshua, represented by the Bridegroom, continues expressing love:

> Your shoots are an orchard of pomegranates with choice fruits, henna with nard plants.
>
> —SONG 4:13

A tree contains some fruit, but an orchard contains much more! Here the Bridegroom is speaking about her super-abundance in Him; she isn't just a tree but "an orchard of pomegranates." Whoever abides in Him bears much fruit. When we feed on God's Word and cling to it, we are like a tree planted by rivers of living water, constantly bearing fruit in every season (Psalm 1).

Verse 15 of Song chapter 4 continues: "You are a *garden spring*, a well of *fresh water*, and *streams flowing* from Lebanon" (emphasis added). I love the nuance in this poetic, prophetic language. He is speaking of three different sources of water.

First He says she is a garden spring. This is water bubbling up from the ground, which speaks to the reality of the indwelling Spirit of Christ. In John 4, Jesus says His life within us becomes a well of water springing up to eternal life. Second, He calls her a well of fresh water. This conveys the idea that we carry a fresh anointing as we abide in Messiah Jesus. It is not stale religion that we carry but everlasting life that is continually bubbling up afresh and anew.

Finally, Jesus says she is like streams flowing from Lebanon. This speaks to the fact that her water is life-giving to both herself and those she encounters.

Grab hold of these realities through prayer:

> *Father, let my love be like springs, wells, and rivers of living water. Jesus, thank You for what You have done for me. Empower me to live as a locked garden enclosed, not allowing anything in that defiles or holding back any part of my life from You. Give me the confidence to completely trust You, to go all the way to the top of the mountain of myrrh. I want to enter fully into a life of frankincense and prayer. I want to overcome as the Shulamite bride did.*
>
> *I ask You to give me understanding of how I am involved in spiritual warfare. Teach me the tactics of the enemy. Show me where I need to close doors and where I need to go on offense, exercising the authority You have given me in Jesus' name over the enemy and the realms of darkness. Thank You that You have given me the victory!*

Chapter 13

AWAKE, O NORTH WIND

B Y THIS TIME, the maiden has abandoned herself to the
King and goes a step further, saying:

Awake, O north wind, and come, wind of the south;
make my garden breathe out fragrance, let its spices be
wafted abroad.

—SONG 4:16

North winds are winds of adversity—they are cold and not
pleasing to the flesh. For a short time I lived in Minnesota,
and I remember going outside in the middle of winter for the
first time. I was far from accustomed to those fierce, freezing
north winds. It felt like they cut right through me—so uncomfortable! I never stood there saying, "Come, freezing winds!"
But that is what the bride does here.

Some fruit can only be produced in our lives by God

bringing us through hard times. Job went through a tremendous season of difficulty where he lost everything and then gained it back. Afterward, he said to the Lord, "I have heard of You by the hearing of the ear; but now my eye sees You" (Job 42:5). He gained a clearer view of God by going through those times of great loss.

You may be going through difficult times right now. You may be in a season of testing. Perhaps you have prayed as the Shulamite bride did, "Lord, whatever it takes." But now you feel those chilly winds blowing, and you're struggling.

James told us that Father God brings various testings and trials into our lives to reveal the quality of our faith and to raise it to the next level. (See James 1:2–4.) And sometimes He uses trials to keep us humble while good things are happening. Paul writes in 2 Corinthians 12:7–10:

> Because of the surpassing greatness of the revelations, for this reason, to keep me from exalting myself, there was given me a thorn in the flesh, a messenger of Satan to torment me—to keep me from exalting myself! Concerning this I implored the Lord three times that it might leave me. And He has said to me, "My grace is sufficient for you, for power is perfected in weakness." Most gladly, therefore, I will rather boast about my weaknesses, so that the power of Christ may dwell in me. Therefore I am well content with weaknesses, with insults, with distresses, with persecutions, with difficulties, for Christ's sake; for when I am weak, then I am strong.

A messenger of Satan was actually sent to Paul as a gift from God to keep Paul from exalting himself. That way God could continue to bless and use him. Paul begged God, "Take this thing away. It's hurting and tormenting me," but God's response was, "My grace is sufficient for you, for power is perfected in weakness." The north wind blew on Paul's life, and God's power was actually being perfected in it. Like him we must pray, "I'm ready, Father God, to go through whatever You have for me as long as it brings me closer to You, and as long as it creates within me a dwelling place for You." With the bride we must say, "Father God, I'm not afraid of anything. Whatever You need to bring me through so that Jesus can be fully manifested in me and through me, I say yes, yes, yes!"

Can you honestly say that right now, beloved one? This is part of being mature. He brings us into the fullness of what He has for us not just by causing the warm, pleasurable south winds to blow upon our lives. He allows north winds to sweep over us, not to hurt us but because something about going through hard times perfects His strength in us as we depend on Him. There are treasures the Holy Spirit wants to impart to us that can only be imparted when we are going through difficult times. His power is perfected in our weakness (2 Cor. 12:9).

Belonging to Him

Those winds have an immediate, positive effect, causing the bride's garden to "breathe out fragrance," as verse 16 says, and causing its spices to be "wafted abroad." In other words, receiving from the Spirit in times of suffering somehow causes a greater sense of God's presence and power to flow from our lives. The Bible says that "the Lord is near to the broken-hearted" (Ps. 34:18), and His nearness can be felt by us and others near us. Clinging to God in our sufferings produces a fragrance pleasing to Christ.

Chapter 4 ends with the maiden crying out, "May my beloved come into his garden and eat its choice fruits!" (v. 16). This is a woman who exists for her husband. And the Bridegroom recognizes this, because we see a wonderful shift in the choice of words He uses to describe her. Nine times in the next verse, Yeshua uses the word *my* to refer to His bride:

> I have come into *my garden, my sister, my bride*; I have gathered *my myrrh* along with *my balsam*. I have eaten *my honeycomb* and *my honey*; I have drunk *my wine* and *my milk*. Eat, friends; drink and imbibe deeply, O lovers.
> —SONG 5:1, EMPHASIS ADDED

You see, she had become His possession. Like all of us who believe, she started her Christian journey with a high degree of self-centeredness. In the initial stages of relationship with Jesus, we often use Him and relate to Him very immaturely. We ask Him to answer our prayers, lead us, bless us, and provide for us. Those are all good things to ask Him for, and He delights in supplying our needs. But when we move into maturity, our relationship with Him shifts, and we no longer see Him as existing only for our good. Rather, we come to understand that we exist primarily for His pleasure. Mature believers live for Yeshua, not just for what He does for them.

The King (Messiah Jesus) detects this shift in her heart, and so He speaks of her more possessively than before: "You are my sister, my garden, my bride." He says it because it's true. Consider again the words of Song 5:1 (emphasis added):

> I have come into *my* garden, *my* sister, *my* bride; I have gathered *my* myrrh along with *my* balsam. I have eaten *my* honeycomb and *my* honey; I have drunk *my* wine and *my* milk.

Now He was getting from her that which He desired. He then beckons:

> Eat, friends; drink and imbibe deeply, O lovers.
> —Song 5:1

When we walk in mature love with Messiah Jesus, we embody Him. He becomes incarnate in us and through us so that those around us receive an impartation of His presence, love, goodness, and beauty through our lives. This is what the King means in this verse when He invites His friends to eat and drink deeply. It is an invitation to receive His presence through the lives of submitted, mature believers. Isn't that an awesome thing? When you go to social gatherings or family events, the life of Yeshua wafts from you like a fragrance. Others can actually partake of Messiah Jesus through our lives. This is a stunning reality.

Joining the Jesus of Gethsemane

A new scene and season unfolds as we continue in chapter 5:

> I was asleep but my heart was awake. A voice! My beloved was knocking: "Open to me, my sister, my darling, my dove, my perfect one! For my head is drenched with dew, my locks with the damp of the night."
> —Song 5:2

Here she is, lying in bed half asleep but with her heart awake to Him. When we sleep, our souls in some mysterious sense hover between the material and immaterial worlds. I believe when we sleep, we are the most vulnerable to spiritual atmospheres. The atmosphere on earth in this age is one of war. My sleep can be very intense in the spirit world. Revelations come to me from time to time, but often in my sleep I sense the attack of the enemy. I sense myself being targeted. I sense myself being put in places where I'm alone, and I sense demonic activity around me. Jesus loves us and ministers to us when we sleep, but that doesn't mean we will only have sweet dreams. We live in a battle zone, and I can testify that it manifests in the realm of sleep.

While the bride sleeps, her heart is awake, and the King comes to her as the Jesus of Gethsemane; that is, He comes as He was the night before His crucifixion when His hair was drenched with the night dew.

He asks His bride to open up to Him, not only as one He blesses with south winds, but as one willing to know Him in the fellowship of His sufferings. He says to her, in essence, "Will you receive Me now and share with Me in the nighttime of my greatest grief?" This "voice" she hears reminds me of Revelation 3:20, where Jesus says, "Behold, I stand at the door and knock; if anyone hears My voice and opens the door, I will come in to him and will dine with him, and he with Me."

Now she has a decision to make. Will she open up and receive the Jesus of Gethsemane? Will she open up to share in His sufferings?

She does!

> I have taken off my dress, how can I put it on again? I
> have washed my feet, how can I dirty them again?
>
> —SONG 5:3

In essence, she is saying, "I have already consecrated myself to You. I refuse to go backward." The bride has taken off the dress that once defiled her. She has given herself over to the King and won't put on the "old dress" of her former behavior again.

It is interesting that in Zechariah 3:3–4, we see the Lord take off the priest's filthy garments and wash him clean. It reads:

> Now Joshua [the high priest] was clothed with filthy gar
> ments and standing before the angel. He [the angel of
> the Lord] spoke and said to those who were standing
> before him, saying, "Remove the filthy garments from
> him." Again he said to him, "See, I have taken your iniq-
> uity away from you and will clothe you with festal robes."

In both these passages, the person involved—the bride in the Song and the high priest, Joshua, in Zechariah (not the Joshua who led the Israelites into the Promised Land)—left behind old, dirty clothes and exchanged them for "festal robes" appropriate for their newly cleansed state and relationship with God. Like the bride, we are called to keep moving forward—even when it may be difficult.

The bride continues:

> My beloved extended his hand through the opening, and
> my feelings were aroused for him.
>
> —SONG 5:4

Messiah releases grace ("extended his hand") to her for the test she is about to encounter, and her heart receives His grace ("my feelings were aroused for him"). She continues:

> I arose to open to my beloved; and my hands dripped with myrrh, and my fingers with liquid myrrh, on the handles of the bolt.
>
> —Song 5:5

Here continues the beautiful depiction of Messiah Jesus supernaturally releasing grace and strength for a season of testing she is about to face. The Lord knows in advance what we are about to go through. Oftentimes before a difficult season, the Lord will release a supernatural grace into our lives to prepare us to endure a challenge around the corner. The Lord knew the Shulamite bride was about to go through rough waters, so He released a supernatural empowerment, which she describes as being anointed with "liquid myrrh."

Faith Over Feelings

When I was a new Christian, I was repeatedly deceived by my emotions. I thought that whatever I was feeling must be from God, and it led me into great deception. When I didn't feel God at all, I wondered where He was. I had to learn to walk by faith and not by feelings.

Do you find yourself up one day and down the next, making your spiritual walk feel like a roller coaster ride? Are you controlled by what you feel and sense rather than by simple faith in the Lord? One of the tests we all must pass through is the test of walking by faith and not by sight—or by feelings.

Another test everyone goes through is that of being rejected.

Jesus was rejected not only by people who didn't know Him but also by family members and people who considered themselves righteous. So you and I will be rejected by strangers and friends alike, and this rejection can serve to fortify us in the power of God—if we let it. Don't get me wrong; rejection hurts. When people reject you, they tend to accuse you and lie about you too. They don't view your relationship with Yeshua as valid.

As you may recall, myrrh is sometimes associated with burial (John 19:39–40). Contemplate that the "myrrh" in chapter 5, verse 5 of the Song may point to our need to die to our own desire to be liked and respected. We learn to continue in faithfulness and love for the Lord while being rejected and spoken of wrongly.

A lot of Christians fail this test and have to take it again and again. They are not willing to be rejected or to suffer mistreatment. They do everything they can to be accepted and affirmed by people around them, though Messiah said no one can be His follower if he is more concerned about being accepted by man than by God. Of course, we're human; we all like to be accepted and loved. But will you stand with Yeshua even when people push you away and shut you out?

> How can you believe, when you receive glory from one another and you do not seek the glory that is from the one and only God?
>
> —JOHN 5:44

For her part, the maiden was loyal to her Bridegroom and withstood a strong test in the north winds by remaining faithful to Him while being rejected. But the north winds continued to blow as the Lord withdrew His presence again:

> I opened to my beloved, but my beloved had turned away and had gone! My heart went out to him as he spoke. I searched for him but I did not find him; I called him but he did not answer me.
>
> —Song 5:6

Then an even more challenging test arose:

> The watchmen who make the rounds in the city found me, they struck me and wounded me; the guardsmen of the walls took away my shawl from me.
>
> —Song 5:7

We too must pass the test of bearing Yeshua's reproach, even within the family of God, if we are to get to the top of the mountain. People will betray us. Fellow believers will gossip about us. We will be "struck" by these words and by other unfair actions. When this happens, will we remain faithful to Jesus, or will we depart from the pathway up the mountain of spices? Will it hurt too much to continue? Will we betray the Lord's and our own integrity? Will we compromise or bend to the opinions of men? Will we be ensnared by fear and in so doing sever our close fellowship with Messiah Jesus?

One easy way to test your tolerance for rejection is to talk about Jesus wherever you go—at the store, at your kids' school, at the gas station, at work, with your neighbors. Everybody has a right to hear your testimony about what Yeshua has done for you. If the person behind the store counter asks how you are doing, say, "Praise God, I'm doing well, thanks to Jesus." I really believe every conversation should have some witness of Jesus. Psalm 34 says His praise should always be on our lips. If you don't like that idea, it may be because you are afraid of being rejected.

These persecutors of the bride didn't just strike her; they took away her shawl, which perhaps represented her honor or place of influence in ministry. Paul writes in Philippians 3 that he had suffered the loss of all things that he might know Yeshua not only in the power of His resurrection but also in the fellowship of His sufferings. Do we feel this way? Do you want to go all the way up the mountain of myrrh with the Jesus of Gethsemane? Will we be like the Shulamite bride, who persists through the aching cold of the north winds?

I invite you to make it your prayer to stay faithful to Yeshua even through trials and tests:

> *Father God, sometimes I don't even know what I am going through, or why. Bring me through the rough times. I need Your help. In some cases, Lord, You seem far away. Sometimes I start to feel offended with You, so I ask You to forgive me and remove that feeling. Wash me and release grace to me in my present situation. Take me through these trials as You promised You would do. Perfect Your power in my weakness. Get me to the top of the mountain, and establish me there.*
>
> *King Jesus, come into Your garden in me and receive pleasure from me. Eat the choice fruits my life has produced. Help me to live as Your possession, to move beyond immaturity, where my spiritual*

journey is about me, and into maturity, where I see that it is all about You. May the King come into His garden.

Jesus, I thank You that the Spirit is transforming me, that You are at work in my life to will and to do for Your good pleasure. I ask You to transform me, Father, into the image of Your Son. Let me become like the Shulamite bride in the Song of Songs. Yeshua, I want to fulfill the destiny for which You created me and the purpose for which You called me, to be totally Yours forever!

Chapter 14

LOVESICK

THE SHULAMITE BRIDE was going through hard times with the suffering Bridegroom, and it seemed as if He had forsaken her. People had rejected her, heaping reproaches and accusations upon her. They "struck" her in hurtful ways. They removed her from her place of influence.

She might have been tempted to doubt her Bridegroom King and ask, "Does He really love me? Is He really with me anymore?" She might have been tempted to become bitter and angry at God. She might have begun to wonder, "Is God even real? Does following Him make any difference?" But in this moment of deep pain and confusion, she did something extraordinary: she turned with humility to the believers around her and asked them for help.

> I adjure you, O daughters of Jerusalem, if you find my beloved, as to what you will tell him: For I am lovesick.
> —SONG 5:8

Rather than nurse a grudge against God, the bride acted with a tender heart, humbly asking the daughters of Jerusalem—those less mature than she—to help her find her Beloved. What a heavenly attitude. She was willing to receive help from anybody in this moment of need. Sometimes you and I don't receive all that God has for us because of pride. We consider certain people less spiritual than we are. That may be true, but when we close our hearts and minds to hearing from God through others, we suffer.

Beloved one, Father God can speak through anybody! He speaks through little children. In the Bible He spoke through a donkey. When we are going through difficult times—in fact, all the time—we should listen for the voice of God in what others say, not ruling it out just because we consider the vessel to be unworthy. I am here to tell you that God speaks through unworthy vessels—of which you and I are prime examples!

Somehow the bride has kept her heart from offense. Her strong love remains kindled and alive, and she tells them openly, "I am lovesick," meaning, "I am so hungry for God. I am so thirsty for God. I can't stop thinking about Him."

The daughters of Jerusalem, stunned by her attitude in the face of such bad treatment, begin to ask tough questions:

> What kind of beloved is your beloved, O most beautiful among women? What kind of beloved is your beloved, that thus you adjure us?
>
> —Song 5:9

In other words, "Is this guy worth it? Why not give up on Him? Why does He treat you like this if He's so great? Why keep following Him? Why put up with all that you've been going through? Look where it got you. Your life is falling apart. You don't deserve this. Find someone who cares for you, protects you, and never leaves you in harm's way." In the world's ears, this all sounds like good advice. You may even have faced questions like these in your own life, from your own friends or family members.

You gave yourself over to Jesus, spent time reading the Bible, went faithfully to church, served others, gave money to support kingdom work, and so on. Maybe family members, coworkers, or friends said, "Why do you do all this? Why spend all your time at church? Why give so much of your money away? You're overdoing it. It's not worth it. You could be using your time, money, and talents on something that pays off better." This is what the Shulamite bride heard from the daughters of Jerusalem.

What she does next, considering the pain the north winds had brought to her, is astonishing: she praises the King to these daughters of Jerusalem in such a way that they feel enraptured by His beauty and glory themselves.

> My beloved is dazzling and ruddy, outstanding among
> ten thousand. His head is like gold, pure gold.
> —Song 5:10–11

Gold speaks of His divine nature, and the head speaks of leadership. Ephesians 1:22–23 says (emphasis added):

> And He [the Father] put all things in subjection under
> His [Jesus'] feet, and gave Him as *head* over all things to
> the church, which is His body, the fullness of Him who
> fills all in all.

Jesus has become our head. As members of the body of Messiah, you and I are connected to Jesus, our head, and His leadership is royal and perfect, like gold. Furthermore, you and I have heads! Our heads—meaning our minds—are likewise supposed to be "gold." We are created to have the mind of Christ. This is why I like to pray: "Lord Jesus, make my thoughts Your thoughts. Cleanse my mind and rewire the way I think so that my head becomes like Your head. I don't want to have natural opinions and think in a natural way. I want to see as You see. Administer Your way of thinking, Your divine life, into my head. Your thoughts, plans, and ways are like pure gold!"

The maiden goes on:

> His locks are like clusters of dates and black as a raven. His eyes are like doves beside streams of water, bathed in milk, and reposed in their setting.
>
> —Song 5:11–12

Have you ever looked into somebody's eyes and seen depths of love, like deep pools of water? That is how she describes the Bridegroom's eyes. They are "beside streams of water," and they are "reposed in their setting," meaning they are eyes of peace, reflecting His settled confidence.

As she continues to exalt the King, she says,

> His cheeks are like a bed of balsam, *banks* of sweet-scented herbs; his lips are lilies dripping with liquid myrrh.
>
> —Song 5:13, emphasis added

Cheeks again represent emotions. "Banks" are places of relaxation and pleasure. His cheeks are not tense but full of sweetness. His face is free of stress. I like to reflect on passages like this as a way to guide my own emotions. We see in her poetic description who God is emotionally. When we compare our own emotions to His, it helps us rein in and redirect our feelings and bring them into agreement with God's. For example, if I am needlessly sad, I begin to declare, "Lord, You are joy, and You live inside me, so I can activate my will and enter into that joy." Not long ago, I heard the Lord clearly speak to me. He said, "Rejoice continually, and you will overcome every obstacle." This lines up with God's written Word that says, "Rejoice in the Lord always" (Phil. 4:4).

In Revelation 4, we read that there is a sea of glass in front of God's throne. A pane of glass is completely flat, so the place around the throne is a place of utter stillness. God is completely at peace, completely relaxed. Sometimes I find myself needlessly elevating my stress levels. Then I think, "Is God stressed? No, He is relaxed." So I slow down, pull my energy back, and release the stress and pride that are producing anxiety in me. Like the Shulamite bride, I want to praise His "cheeks," the beauty and perfection of His emotions. The best way for us to honor His emotions is to bring ours into alignment with His.

Our Strong Pillar

Chapter 5 of the Song ends with the Shulamite bride saying:

His hands are rods of gold set with beryl; his abdomen
is carved ivory inlaid with sapphires. His legs are pillars

of alabaster set on pedestals of pure gold; his appearance is like Lebanon choice as the cedars. His mouth is full of sweetness. And he is wholly desirable. This is my beloved and this is my friend, O daughters of Jerusalem.
—Song 5:14–16

She praises His abdomen, speaking of His rock-like inner nature. She praises His legs, speaking of His authority over the earth. Then she concludes by saying, "And he is wholly desirable." She makes Him sound so beautiful to the daughters of Jerusalem that their perspective completely shifts from them questioning her sanity in following Him to now saying, "We want to go with you to find this man!"

Where has your beloved gone, O most beautiful among women? Where has your beloved turned, that we may seek him with you?
—Song 6:1

The Shulamite bride, this shadow of the church, has the power to lift Jesus up in such a way as to change the spiritual atmospheres around her and draw others to Him. This is our power too, beloved one! In praising Him and speaking of His glory, we displace the power of the enemy and replace it with the attractiveness of our Bridegroom King.

Notice the bride draws people to Jesus not by condemning them, not by telling them how immature they are, but by telling them how beautiful He is. We too can tell others: "He is so beautiful. He is so victorious. Not only does He wash away all our sins, but He anoints us with the beauty and fragrance of God. Jesus has touched my life in ways no human could do. He has changed my heart. I want you to know that Jesus is so excellent that He will satisfy you like nothing on earth can. Give yourself to Messiah Jesus and you too will experience the greatness of His love!"

Are you ready to testify like that if someone asks about your relationship with Yeshua? People are curious and ready to listen. Have you ever described Jesus to someone else with such passion and richness they said, "I have to go to church with you! Invite me to your Bible study—I'll come!"

When we testify, some people will react as the daughters of Jerusalem did in the Song and say, "Where has your beloved gone, O most beautiful among women? Where has your beloved turned, that we may seek him with you?" (Song 6:1).

Once again, the Shulamite bride has an answer ready:

> My beloved has gone down to his garden, to the beds of balsam, to pasture his flock in the gardens and gather lilies.
>
> —SONG 6:2

A powerful truth is revealed here: the place to find Jesus is in serving. Yeshua said, "The Son of Man did not come to be served, but to serve, and to give His life a ransom for many" (Matt. 20:28). If you and I as mature believers are going to experience Messiah Jesus in a deeper way, as I said earlier, we won't do it just by sitting in our bedrooms listening to worship music all day long. That's an awesome thing to do, but as we mature, a vital connection comes as we serve by working alongside Him in the garden.

Jesus, knowing that the Father had given all things into His hands, and that He had come forth from God and was going back to God, got up from supper, and laid aside His garments; and taking a towel, He girded Himself. Then He poured water into the basin, and began to wash the disciples' feet and to wipe them with the towel with which He was girded....

So when He had washed their feet, and taken His garments and reclined at the table again, He said to them... You call Me Teacher and Lord; and you are right, for so I am. If I then, the Lord and the Teacher, washed your feet, you also ought to wash one another's feet. For I gave you an example that you also should do as I did to you.

—JOHN 13:3–5, 12–15

If you wonder why others seem to get so much out of their spiritual walks while yours feels drab and dreary, lack of serving is likely part of the reason. Be a servant in your relationship with others. Be a servant in your local church body. If you ask the Lord and don't get clear direction where to serve, my advice is simply to start somewhere. Pick a ministry at your church. People often fall into their places of service over time, but you must step out. Don't wait for a divine voice to give you specific direction. Look for needs and meet them, both in your relationships in general and in your local church body. You will have a more vibrant, interesting, and close experience of Yeshua.

The maiden then affirms,

I am my beloved's and my beloved is mine, *he who pastures his flock among the lilies.*

—SONG 6:3, EMPHASIS ADDED

She is now totally partnered with Him. She is on earth to serve with Him in the garden, the field, the vineyard of His church. The north winds of rejection, persecution, and reproach cannot separate her from Him. She has passed a critical test.

May it be our prayer to pass this same test.

> *Lord, I pray that You will give us the heart of the Shulamite bride! Help us to invite Your testing, and help us to fall more deeply in love with You even as the freezing north winds blow. Lord, when people treat us unfairly, striking us with their words and even removing us from places of influence, I ask that our hearts would grow sweeter rather than bitter. Let us praise You to everyone around us with such sincerity and insight that they too will want to know our excellent King. Thank You for hearing and answering our cries.*

Chapter 15

BRIGHTER LIKE THE DAWN

A s we've seen throughout this book, the Song is a dialogue between the Bridegroom, representing Yeshua, and His bride, which is a shadow of the church, as they journey together into divine love. At this point in this holy voyage the Bridegroom continues to affirm His bride:

> You are as beautiful as *Tirzah*, my darling, as lovely as *Jerusalem*, as awesome as an army with banners.
> —Song 6:4, emphasis added

In the ancient world Tirzah was reputed to be the most beautiful city of all. In fact, many of the ancient Israeli kings were buried there. Think of the most attractive city you know, or imagine a beautiful nature scene. Maybe you love to dream about the beaches of Hawaii or Florida, or the mountains of Colorado. The way that special place makes you feel is how

Tirzah is used symbolically here. Messiah says His bride is more beautiful than the most attractive places on earth—more beautiful than waterfalls, forests of trees, fields of flowers, breathtaking mountainscapes. Considering all the places on earth, His bride is still more beautiful to Him.

Further, He says she is as lovely as Jerusalem, and that is perhaps the highest compliment of all because Jerusalem is the city of the great King (Matt. 5:35). It is the city where God's glory dwelled and where Jesus will return to rule the earth. That is high praise! You are beautiful to Him.

In the same verse He then praises her for her conquering power, saying she is "as awesome as an army with banners." When an army in the ancient world won a victory, they would return to their hometown with their victory banner waving above their heads. They had come back from war. They had defeated the enemy. They had conquered the foe, and they were triumphant. Jesus compares this to the personal accomplishments of His bride; she had not swung a sword, but she had conquered her fears. She had conquered her dependence on feelings and comfort. She had conquered the intimidation that can come from the rejection of people. And she had conquered her love of self over her love of God. She had conquered everything that stood between her and the Bridegroom. Remember that He had appeared to her on the mountaintop, which is a place of having conquered.

When you and I conquer hindrances and hurdles on the pathway up the mountain of myrrh, Jesus sees us too as valiant and victorious, like an army marching home under divine banners. It is an amazing reality.

"Turn Away"

If we believe the Song of Songs is a prophetic love story about our relationship with Messiah Jesus, then we must recognize that what comes next in chapter 6 is one of the most mysterious and humbling verses in all of God's Word. The Bridegroom, Messiah Jesus, says to the bride:

> Turn your eyes away from me, for they have confused me.
>
> —SONG 6:5

The King James reads, "Turn your eyes away from me, for they have overwhelmed me." How should we take this? Is Yeshua really saying He can be "confused" or even "overwhelmed" by us? The Bible is using anthropomorphic language here, meaning it's explaining something in human terms so we can understand. Anthropomorphic language is when God speaks of Himself as being human so we can relate to Him even though, obviously, God is not human but divine. Even as we can be overwhelmed when we experience somebody massively loving us, Yeshua is described in this poetic Song as being overwhelmed when He sees God's love released through His bride.

The way the Song portrays it is that Yeshua could hardly stare directly into her eyes because of the piercing beauty of God now shining from her. This is not out of weakness; it is poetic language. Maybe you have experienced looking into somebody's eyes, and what you saw was so beautiful, clear, and strong that the only appropriate thing to do was glance to the side. It can be almost overwhelming. I know it is inconceivable that we could have that type of effect on Messiah, but I kind of get it. Remember, Yeshua is the very essence of humility, and He has voluntarily placed Himself in a position where He can be touched by us. He has willingly made Himself vulnerable to us.

The Bridegroom continues to praise her, from the top of her head to the bottoms of her feet. Beloved one, it is worth repeating that this is who you are; you are the bride of Jesus, beautiful to Him from crown to sole, and nobody can ever take that away from you. Age can't rob you of this reality. Neither can death or disease. You will always be beautiful to God! Being human, we need to hear the same praise over and over. Our perfect Bridegroom knows this and is faithful to tell us more than once how beautiful we are to Him. Thank You, Lord Jesus!

After praising her beauty, He says:

> There are sixty queens and eighty concubines, and maidens without number; but my dove, my perfect one, is unique: she is her mother's only daughter; she is the pure child of the one who bore her.
>
> —SONG 6:8–9

In essence, Jesus is saying, "There are many amazing people—sixty queens and eighty concubines—but you are unique. You are not like the rest. You are my favorite because there is no one like you." We are all God's best—His favorites—because each one of us is unique. Nobody else on earth can compare to you! The Lord relates to each one of us individually, just as a parent does with a child. Good parents never make their children feel like there is a favorite but rather let each child know he or she is special.

Brightening Glory

The Song continues:

> The maidens saw her and called her blessed, the queens
> and the concubines also, and they praised her, saying,
> "Who is this that *grows like the dawn*, as beautiful as the
> full *moon*, as pure as the *sun*, as awesome as an army
> with banners?"
>
> —SONG 6:9–10, EMPHASIS ADDED

The sun and moon both give off light, though we know the moonlight is the sun's light reflected. The sun shines by day, the moon by night, and the two bodies illuminate the natural world. Jesus uses this natural picture to say that we are being transformed even as the coming of the dawn, which gets brighter until it reaches full day. As the light of the sun reflects off the moon, and as the pure light of the sun shines in its strength, Yeshua says we are growing and being transformed into the very image of God. We are being changed, beloved ones, from strength to strength and from glory to glory.

In 2 Corinthians 3:18, Paul writes about this aspect of being transformed and growing into the light of God: "But we all, with unveiled face, beholding as in a mirror the glory of the Lord, are being transformed into the same image from glory to glory, just as from the Lord, the Spirit." Each one of us, and all of us collectively, are like the Shulamite bride. We are growing as the dawn and bringing illumination to the earth, like the sun and moon.

Serving in the Orchards

At this point, the maiden speaks, saying:

> I went down to the orchard of nut trees to see the blossoms of the valley, to see whether the vine had budded or the pomegranates had bloomed.
>
> —Song 6:11

Once again we see that Jesus is building His kingdom in the orchard and vineyard. So she follows Him to serve and build with Him. The bride wants "to see the blossoms of the valley, to see whether the vine had budded or the pomegranates had bloomed." In beautiful, pastoral language she says she wants to be where the church is being built. She desires now to go into the orchard and into the vineyard to see God's "plants" growing.

Have you ever visited a church just because you were curious to see what that local congregation looked and acted like as a unique expression within the body of Messiah? That is the picture here. The Shulamite bride wanted to see and assess the life and vibrancy of the church, Messiah's expression, up close. She took great pleasure in the blossoms, buds, and blooms she encountered there.

Then something unexpected happened.

> Before I was aware, my soul set me over the chariots of my noble people.
>
> —Song 6:12

In other words, when she went down to the place where God was building His kingdom, suddenly her soul rose up within her like a nobleman over the people. It rose up to help them, to strengthen them, to pour love into them because now she was strong and willing. She had overcome and grown from glory to glory. She had ascended to the top of the mountain. Down in the nut orchard where God's people were still growing, many were weak and needing help as she once needed it. A noble impulse impelled her to lay down her life to serve others, to be used of God to partner with Him for the building of His kingdom. She knew she had the strength to help them. She knew she had something in her to impart, and so she was moved to choose to serve.

The Dance

The voices of others now intrude into her commitment.

> Come back, come back, O Shulammite; come back, come back, that we may gaze at you!
>
> —SONG 6:13

They are crying: "Come back to us. Don't leave us. We want you here. Don't go serve on the mission field. Don't spend so much time in the vineyard. We need you here. Let's keep things as they were. We liked you better that way!" As you rise up in confidence and capability as the bride did, many people will want to hold you back.

Another group responds:

> Why should you gaze at the *Shulammite*, as at the dance of *the two companies*?
>
> —SONG 6:13, EMPHASIS ADDED

The "two companies" speaks to the two types of responses to the bride leaving the familiar place and going to minister and serve in the kingdom. One response came from those she was leaving behind. Some of these sincerely loved her, appreciated the anointing that was on her, and received from her life. But a second group said the opposite: "Good riddance! We've had enough of your Jesus talk. We're done hearing you talk about the Bible and sing those praise songs all day. Let her go." This is the Holy Spirit's portrait of what happens whenever a person becomes sold out for Jesus.

A dance of two camps takes place. One camp is inspired by our zeal and God's work in our lives, and they want to partake of it and be with us. The other camp wants us to leave. Yeshua warned that this would happen. He said of Himself, "Do not think that I came to bring peace on the earth; I did not come to bring peace, but a sword. For I came to set a man against his father, and a daughter against her mother, and a daughter-in-law against her mother-in-law; and a man's enemies will be the members of his household" (Matt. 10:34–36).

When we get radical for Jesus, our lives will bring division just as we see the Shulamite bride's life brought division when she became radical for the Bridegroom. If you are lukewarm, you will not bring division. But Jesus also said, "Woe to you when all men speak well of you, for their fathers used to treat the false prophets in the same way" (Luke 6:26). Only lukewarm people draw universal praise in this world. If people don't divide in response to your life, it simply means you are not sold out for Jesus. You are not passionate. You need to press in to Him and go all the way as the Shulamite bride did. Everybody in our lives should know who we are living for. Everybody should know we love Jesus with everything we have.

Interestingly, this is the only time in the Song of Songs that the bride is called "the Shulamite." Consider this: the name Solomon in Hebrew is "Shlomo," which derives from *shalom*, the word for peace. The name they gave the Shulamite bride here also is related to the Hebrew word for peace. In other words, the names of Solomon and the Shulamite bride both come from the same root Hebrew word meaning "peace."

We take on the name and character of the King we serve. Jesus, the Prince of Peace, has given us His name! Just as when a bride takes the name of her bridegroom and lets go of her last name upon being married, we prophetically take on the identity and character of the One we "marry" in the Spirit. This is a profound truth!

I encourage you to invite the Lord to make this revelation come alive in your heart:

> *Father, I ask You to show me my noble calling laboring in Your orchards, Your fields, Your vineyards, among Your people. Lord, take me to the mountaintop where I overcome, then down to the places of harvest where Your children grow. Give me the selfless heart of the Shulamite bride, and build in me the warrior spirit she possessed to never be stopped in her progress. Jesus, You said You would build Your church and the gates of hell would not prevail against it. Put Your conquering Spirit in me so I cannot be stopped or pushed back. Because You have risen from the dead, I will triumph. I declare I*

am more than a conqueror through Him who loved me (Rom. 8:37).

Finally, let me hear Your affirming voice even as You affirmed the Shulamite bride at many points during her journey. Remind me how beautiful I am to You, and let this give me the confidence and courage I need to continue to climb and reach the very top of the mountain. Having conquered, let me shine forth like the sun and the moon, as awesome as a victorious army marching with its banners. Amen!

Chapter 16

YOU ARE BEAUTIFUL
AND DELIGHTFUL

C HAPTER 7 OF the Song presents sensual language, which is one reason we often don't hear it taught in church services!

It reads:

"How beautiful are your feet in sandals, O prince's daughter! The curves of your hips are like jewels, the work of the hands of an artist. Your navel is like a round goblet which never lacks mixed wine; your belly is like a heap of wheat fenced about with lilies. Your two breasts are like two fawns, twins of a gazelle.

"Your neck is like a tower of ivory, your eyes like the pools in Heshbon by the gate of Bath-rabbim; your nose is like the tower of Lebanon, which faces toward Damascus. Your head crowns you like Carmel, and the flowing locks of your head are like purple threads; the king is captivated by your tresses. How beautiful and how delightful you are, my love, with all your charms!

"Your stature is like a palm tree, and your breasts are like its clusters. I said, 'I will climb the palm tree, I will take hold of its fruit stalks.' Oh, may your breasts be like clusters of the vine, and the fragrance of your breath like apples, and your mouth like the best wine!"

"It goes down smoothly for my beloved, flowing gently through the lips of those who fall asleep."

—SONG 7:1–9

As we have seen, this is a prophetic love song written in anthropomorphic language, meaning God is expressing Himself in human terms to convey to us a reality too big to fully understand with human language. The most intimate way of knowing and loving somebody in earthly relationships is in sexual union. We see this, for example, in Genesis 4:1 and 25, which say Adam "knew" his wife after experiencing sexual intercourse with her. So the most profound way we can experience intimacy in the natural world is through the sexual union that happens in a married relationship.

But let me say strongly, this Song is not about a sexual union with God. It is simply a way of helping us understand how deep and intimate God's love is for us.

God Loves How We Are Made

There is another important application that is very meaningful for me. As we see Jesus praising His bride here in chapter 7, it tells us that God cares about our bodies. Sometimes we are inclined to think Father God loves our souls and spirits but is not really concerned about our bodies. But that is a fallacy and not true. He made our bodies, and the Bible calls them "fearfully and wonderfully made" (Ps. 139:14). When we are physically sick, God cares. When we are in pain, our plight touches Him. Father God's love is thorough and extends to every part of us, including our physical bodies.

Jesus Himself took on a physical body (John 1:14). We need to stop rejecting our bodies and acting like they are part of the curse. No! God made your body! We all have aches and pains and things we struggle with pertaining to our physical beings—but God never hates our bodies. He wants to release His healing virtue to repair and restore them so they too reflect His glory. After He made man, He "blessed them" and said, "Behold, it is very good." (See Genesis 1:28, 31.)

We need to love, nurture, and bless our bodies. Take me, for instance. I always wished I were taller. I stand five-foot-six, and that's on my tiptoes. But I am not going to curse my body. God made me this height, and I am not going to agree with the devil and curse God's choices. No, I'm going to say, "Father God, thank You for making me the way You did." I like to turn it into a joke because I heard that archaeologists say the average Jewish person at the time Jesus lived was between five feet four inches and five feet six inches. Based on that, I like to say I am created in Jesus' likeness!

What I am trying to help you understand is that Messiah Jesus' love for us encompasses our physical beings. Some of you reading this have inferiority complexes and are not receiving the love of God for your physical bodies. In a manner of speaking, you are cursing your body. But God does not curse your body—ever. We need to bless our bodies regardless of how they function or what they look like. I understand that there are parts of our bodies we wish were different either in appearance or function. One day we will have new, glorified bodies, but for now we must bless and nurture the bodies we have. As you bless your body, you will live in better health and greater freedom in the Spirit.

So Yeshua blesses the Shulamite bride's body. He blesses her feet. He blesses her navel. He blesses her eyes. He blesses her head, and so forth.

The Lord blesses your body too. Let's agree in prayer right now to receive this truth:

> Father, I thank You for my physical body. It is a vessel of honor and glory for You to dwell in. Come and strengthen my physical heart, my lungs, my arteries, and my blood. Come and strengthen my legs and arms. Come and strengthen my nervous system. Thank You, Lord Jesus, for loving me from head to toe. I say that I am fearfully and wonderfully made. I thank You for this earthen vessel You have given me in which to carry Your anointing while I am on earth. And I thank You that one day I will have a new heavenly body that will work even better and is indeed perfect and ageless! In Yeshua's name and for Yeshua's fame, amen.

He Desires Us

Another mystifying verse is Song 7:9, where the Bridegroom says to His bride, "Your mouth like the best wine." To this she replies, "It goes down smoothly for my beloved, flowing gently through the lips of those who fall asleep." We can apply this in a very practical way. When we are struggling to obey God in something He has asked us to do, we can confess by faith, "Your wine goes down smoothly. I will obey You."

First John 5:3 says God's commandments are not burdensome. We must come to a place in life where we are not choking on His will. We want to be like the bride, who said of God's will for her life, "It goes down smoothly." We have no right to treat His commandments as if they are a big chore. When we are strengthened and perfected in love, we say yes to Father God, yes to His will, and confess, "Your will is smooth and pleasant, not burdensome."

For instance, if the Lord nudges you to witness to somebody in public, rather than hem and haw and struggle and resist, say, "Father, I will obey You. This task is not a burden to me because Your wine goes down smoothly." Beloved one, the Song of Songs is more than a poetic book; it unlocks practical application for our lives today!

I am also encouraged by the last part of verse 9: "...flowing gently through the lips of those who fall asleep." Here I see Messiah Jesus reminding us that His love flows gently to us even when we're sleeping. That doesn't mean our dreams will always be sweet. We are in a war. "We do not wrestle against flesh and blood," Paul says, "but against principalities, against powers, against the rulers of the darkness of this age, against spiritual hosts of wickedness in the heavenly places" (Eph. 6:12, NKJV).

We are in a spiritual battle, beloved one, but God is protecting us in the midst of the fight. Psalm 4:8 says, "In peace I will both lie down and sleep, for You alone, O LORD, make me to dwell in safety." Like the Shulamite bride, we can have confidence that whether we are awake or asleep, Yeshua's love surrounds and protects us.

A Turning Point

Notice the subtle nuance of verse 10, when the Shulamite declares:

> I am my beloved's, and his desire is for me.

Gone is her prior statement, "He is mine." That is still true, but her focus is not on possessing Him for her own benefit, but on Him possessing her for His benefit. Her perspective has changed. Her beautiful journey has brought her to maturity.

She knows without a hint of doubt that the King desires her. She is completely secure in this fact. The Lord wants us to understand that He desires us too. Some of us have a hard time believing this because the devil has used shame, guilt, self-contempt, and accusation to keep us from believing that God desires us. When we reject ourselves, it renders us incapable of receiving the love of God. If we can't accept ourselves, we can't receive the love of another.

Some reading this are struggling to receive love. You must be able to say and believe, "His desire is for me." Come into agreement with Father God right now. Nothing in all of creation is as beautiful to Him as you are. We are the pinnacle of His creation, and He made *us* in His own image. The Spirit of Messiah Jesus Himself, who is ultimate beauty, lives in you. You can't help but be wholly desirable to God!

If you've been struggling to accept the fact that you are

beautiful and that God desires you, let Messiah wash that self-rejection off you and bring you out of darkness. Let Him reveal how much He loves you so that, like the Shulamite bride, you will be able to say with confidence, "He desires me!"

Eager to Work

Being fully convinced the Bridegroom loves and desires her, and that she is altogether lovely to Him, the bride says:

> Come, my beloved, let *us* go out into the *country*, let us spend the night in the *villages*. Let us rise early and go to the vineyards; let us see whether the vine has budded and its blossoms have opened, and whether the pomegranates have bloomed. There I will give you my love.
> —Song 7:11–12, emphasis added

She is so free in His love, she is released to focus on serving others. And notice that she says four times in these two verses, "Let us..." This tells us she is in partnership with the King. She is co-laboring with Him to reach everybody—those in the country and in the villages.

Jesus revealed the connection between loving Him and working for Him in His conversation with Peter in John 21. Three times Yeshua asks Peter if he loves Him, and three times He instructs Peter to show it by tending His lambs and feeding His sheep. He was telling Peter in essence, "If you really love Me, give Me your love by tending My lambs and shepherding My sheep. Love Me by doing the work of building My church." This is what the Shulamite bride said she was going to do. She was going into the vineyard to give the King her love there.

This applies directly to you and me. If we want to love Jesus in the most profound way, we must serve Him. Whether it's volunteering in the nursery, helping in the maintenance of the facility, preparing meals, calling people on the phone to pray with them, or preaching the gospel, we can each find somewhere to love Jesus by doing the work of building His kingdom.

This is what the Shulamite bride did. As she grew in divine love, she went from one who was focused only on receiving Yeshua's love to one who instead was focused on giving Him love by ministering to others. She had made up her mind to spend the rest of her life building God's kingdom.

Then she says:

> The mandrakes have given forth fragrance; and over our doors are all choice fruits, both new and old, which I have saved up for you, my beloved.
>
> —Song 7:13

Mandrakes were the love plants in the Bible. The Shulamite bride is saying that the Bridegroom's fragrance is exuding from her. His love is coming forth from her as she loves Him by tending to and building His kingdom. Her life is bearing fruit. Over her doors "are all choice fruits, both new and old." Everything about her life speaks of His love, just as the fragrance of mandrakes do. She has truly been gloriously transformed.

I invite you to pray that these dynamic spiritual truths will become the reality of your life:

Father God, I bless this earthly body You gave me to be Your temple. I speak life to my body. Thank You for building into my body the divine knowledge to create antibodies to combat sickness. I also thank You that one day I will receive a glorious body in which there are no aches or pains, sicknesses or struggles.

Lord Jesus, I say boldly that You desire me. I belong to You. I am eager to join You in the fields of harvest—in the gardens, orchards, and vineyards of Your kingdom work. I thank You that You enjoy working with me and that You offer me the unspeakable privilege of co-laboring with You in the building of Your kingdom. Fill my life with the abundant fruit and evidence of our mature, mutual love.

Chapter 17

PUT A SEAL OVER MY HEART

Now we come to the last chapter of the Song, in which we find the Shulamite bride saying to the Bridegroom:

Oh that you were like a brother to me who nursed at my mother's breasts. If I found you outdoors, I would kiss you; no one would despise me, either.

—Song 8:1

She is so passionate for her Bridegroom husband that she thinks it would be frowned upon if she were to express it publicly. Maybe you know what it's like to feel great love for the Lord inside, but you feel hindered in expressing it. Even during worship services, some people are uncomfortable raising their hands; their love is confined. The bride says that her love for the Bridegroom is so strong and heated that if she were to show the fullness of it in public, people would not understand. They would get the wrong idea.

She says in the next verse:

> I would lead you and bring you into the house of my mother, who used to instruct me; I would give you spiced wine to drink from the juice of my pomegranates.
>
> —Song 8:2

Here the bride is saying she wants to have open fellowship with the King around the table of her mother and those closest to her, and she wants to honor Him there by giving Him spiced wine in their presence.

After my mother passed away, we observed the shiva, which is a seven-day period after a loved one passes when family and friends come and comfort those who were closest to the deceased, particularly the spouse and children. While we were sitting shiva, I had an opportunity to see people I hadn't spoken with in thirty years, and I was able to tell them all about what Yeshua had done and was doing in my life. What an opportunity it was to share Messiah Jesus with some I had not seen in many years, "in the home" of the one who conceived me.

Absorbed in divine romance, the lovers continue:

> "Let his left hand be under my head and his right hand embrace me."
>
> "I want you to swear, O daughters of Jerusalem, do not arouse or awaken my love until she pleases."
>
> —Song 8:3–4

She is secure and resting in His love.

Then the scene shifts, and the Holy Spirit speaks these words through the Bridegroom:

> Who is this coming up from the wilderness leaning on her beloved?
>
> —SONG 8:5

In a powerful and deeply personal moment for the bride, the Holy Spirit looks at her and marvels as she comes up from the wilderness leaning on her Bridegroom (Yeshua). Because the two have become united together, she has emerged in victory. This moment awaits each one of us. Just as Yeshua led the Shulamite bride out of the wilderness into triumph on the mountaintop, so He leads you and me. Each one of us comes up from our own unique wildernesses as overcomers, leaning on Jesus.

It calls to mind one of my favorite scriptures, Psalm 40:2–3. There the psalmist expresses gratitude to the Lord for saving him from the miry clay. He was about to be swallowed up by the circumstances of life, but he said, "He set my feet upon a rock making my footsteps firm. He put a new song in my mouth, a song of praise to our God." I love that psalm because that's what God did for me—and He will do the same for you.

Now the bride's journey has gone full circle. The Bridegroom brings her mind back to the beginning of their journey:

> Beneath the apple tree I awakened you; there your mother was in labor with you, there she was in labor and gave you birth.
>
> —SONG 8:5

The last time we found the bride under the apple tree was in chapter 2. Jesus awakened her there and is now reminding her of that marking encounter. He recalls the beginning of her journey in divine love and refers to her being born of the Holy Spirit, saying, "There your mother was in labor and gave you birth."

The Strong Seal of Love

She never wants their relationship to end. Figuratively wrapping her arms around her Bridegroom, the lover explains:

> Put me like a seal over your heart, like a seal on your arm.
> For love is as strong as death, jealousy is as severe as Sheol;
> its flashes are flashes of fire, the very flame of the LORD.
> —Song 8:6

The seal she speaks of here is what has been accomplished in her. "Let it not be diluted or compromised," she says. "Let no man deceive me. Guard what we have gained."

The Holy Spirit is the one who seals us, forever deepening our experience of God. The bride is prophetically pointing to the baptism of the Holy Spirit, which is a baptism of fire and love. Some people regard the baptism of the Holy Spirit as a once-in-a-lifetime experience, but the reality is that the baptism of the Holy Spirit is not just a one-time experience because the effects of it are progressive. It keeps changing and transforming us in deeper and deeper ways over time. Love is inexhaustible.

The bride's words here remind me of what Yeshua said in Revelation 3:11: "I am coming quickly; hold fast what you have, so that no one will take your crown."

And so the bride calls out to the Bridegroom, Jesus, "Place

me as a seal on Your heart for Your love is stronger than death."
Yeshua rose from the grave and conquered death, and His jealousy is stronger than both.

> Many waters cannot quench love, nor will rivers overflow it.
>
> —SONG 8:7

In the natural world, water puts out fire. But in the spirit, no water, no trial, no temptation can put out the fire of God's supernatural love. Nothing can overwhelm you. "Neither death, nor life, nor angels, nor principalities, nor things present, nor things to come, nor powers, nor height, nor depth, nor any other created thing, will be able to separate us from the love of God" (Rom. 8:38–39). The love of God is the strongest force that exists. It just keeps going deeper and wider and higher. We're never going to exhaust Yeshua's love because He always has more to give. Many waters cannot put out its flame.

> If a man were to give all the riches of his house for love,
> it would be utterly despised.
>
> —SONG 8:7

Nothing in existence even remotely compares to the value of God's love for us in Christ Jesus! No worldly thing holds a candle to it. The greatest earthly riches are garbage in comparison to the love of God. The love of God is precious and beautiful and powerful beyond words of description. It just keeps rolling over us in waves, bringing us into deeper and deeper depths.

The Little Sister

Then the Shulamite bride says something seemingly mysterious:

> We have a little sister, and she has no breasts; what shall
> we do for our sister on the day when she is spoken for?
> —SONG 8:8

This little sister represents other believers who are less mature than she is. That's why the little sister has no breasts. The bride is concerned about those less mature than she. The Shulamite bride has become mature in love and concerned about the welfare of other people. So she asks Yeshua, "What are we going to do for her? I want her to be fully blessed and have a great reward."

She continues:

> If she is a *wall*, we will build on her a battlement of silver; but
> if she is a *door*, we will barricade her with planks of cedar.
> —SONG 8:9, EMPHASIS ADDED

In this context, a wall is a person who has strength. The Shulamite bride describes herself in the next verse as a wall. A wall is able to stand against the enemy. A wall is able to protect. The Shulamite bride asks the Lord to strengthen her little sister's wall.

But in the case of a little sister who is "a door," the bride wants to barricade her, or surround her, with planks of cedar. A door is an opening. It indicates someone so immature in the faith that she has no defenses against darkness. Rather, she is like an infant, completely vulnerable to anything that happens to it. If the little sister is just a door—totally open, vulnerable, and without protection—she needs to be surrounded so she will be kept safe.

Then the Shulamite bride describes herself:

> I was a wall, and my breasts were like towers; then I became in his eyes as one who finds peace.
>
> —SONG 8:10

She was declaring her strength and ability to stand against darkness. Breasts are instruments that nurture. She describes her breasts as "towers." This means she is mature and strong enough to nurture others. It may sound proud, but she was simply agreeing with God about her identity. It is not humble to walk around bemoaning that we are wretched, worthless people. That's not biblical or pleasing to God. We can have a sane estimation of ourselves and say as Paul did, "But by the grace of God I am what I am" (1 Cor. 15:10).

The Shulamite bride has reached the place of knowing she is a strong wall. She knows she can nurture other people. I love what Hebrews 11:5 says about Enoch: "He was not found because God took him up; *for he obtained the witness that before his being taken up he was pleasing to God*" (emphasis added). God does not call us to go through life speaking false humilities over ourselves. When the Lord affirms us and tells us we are beautiful to Him, it is not humble to say we are ugly; that's a lie. It is actually pride, because it shows we are not listening to Messiah but relying on our own perspectives. When Yeshua tells us we are beautiful and we affirm that, we come into agreement with our Creator.

Solomon's Vineyard

The Song goes on to say:

> Solomon had a vineyard at Baal-hamon; he *entrusted the vineyard to caretakers.* Each one was to bring a thousand shekels of silver for its fruit. My very own vineyard is at my disposal; the thousand shekels are for you, Solomon, and two hundred are for those who take care of its fruit.
> —SONG 8:11–12, EMPHASIS ADDED

What's going on here prophetically? Once again, Solomon is a type of King Jesus, and the vineyard is the kingdom of God. In Matthew 21, among other places in the Gospels, Yeshua likens the kingdom of God to a vineyard. Jesus told a parable about a landowner "who planted a vineyard and put a wall around it and dug a wine press in it, and built a tower, and rented it out to vine-growers and went on a journey. When the harvest time approached, he sent his slaves to the vine-growers to receive his produce" (Matt. 21:33–34).

The landowner expected to receive a harvest, just as the king in the Song "entrusted the vineyard to caretakers" and expected each one "to bring a thousand shekels of silver for its fruit." Beloved one, King Jesus expects our lives to bear fruit. Consider Luke 13:6–9:

> And He began telling this parable: "A man had a fig tree which had been planted in his vineyard; and he came looking for fruit on it and did not find any. And he said to the vineyard-keeper, 'Behold, for three years I have come looking for fruit on this fig tree without finding any. Cut it down! Why does it even use up the ground?'

And he answered and said to him, 'Let it alone, sir, for this year too, until I dig around it and put in fertilizer; and if it bears fruit next year, fine; but if not, cut it down.'"

Each of us is going to stand before the judgment seat of God, and He's going to ask us how we used the resources He gave us (2 Cor. 5:10).

Like the Shulamite bride, who was giving her love to the King in the vineyard, Yeshua expects us to use our gifts, talents, time, and treasure serving others and building His kingdom.

In verse 12, the bride proclaims: "My very own vineyard is at my disposal; the thousand shekels are for you, Solomon, and two hundred are for those who take care of its fruit." Her life is bountifully productive. It is a pleasing sacrifice to the King that is absorbed with ministering to His people.

And now as we near the end of our journey, we can hear the King's continuing love for His bride in His next words.

O you who sit in the gardens, *my companions are listening* for your voice—let me hear it!
—SONG 8:13, EMPHASIS ADDED

Notice where the Shulamite bride is at the very end of her life: sitting in the garden. This means she is still serving, still laboring for the King in His vineyard. That is what God desires and expects of us: to devote our lives to building His kingdom.

His "companions"—those who belong to the Bridegroom—were ready and waiting to hear the bride's voice. They needed her help. They were ready to learn from her. Likewise, there are those out there who need to learn from you. They need to hear your voice, just as the companions of the Bridegroom needed to hear the voice of the Shulamite bride.

So Jesus invites her to call out and share freely what He has done for her and taught her in the different seasons of her life. He is telling her, "My people want to draw from the treasures of your life, things old and new. Let me hear it!"

The Climax

Amazingly, stunningly, and profoundly, the final line of the Song foreshadows the return of King Jesus as the bride calls out to Him to come:

> Hurry, my beloved and *come quickly*, like a gazelle or a young stag [taking me home] on the mountains of spices.
> —SONG 8:14, AMP, EMPHASIS ADDED

Now consider this incredible conclusion to the Song of Songs in light of these words from the final chapter of the New Testament:

> Behold, *I am coming quickly*, and My reward is with Me, to render to every man according to what he has done.
> —REVELATION 22:12, EMPHASIS ADDED

I want to ask you to stop for a second and think about this with me. The last verse in the Song is nothing less than a call for the Bridegroom, Messiah, to return and expresses the same yearning we see at the very end of the Book of Revelation, where "the Spirit and the bride say, 'Come'" (Rev. 22:17). The climax of both the Song of Songs and the New Testament is the King's return.

I don't know about you, but this knocks me out!

Notice too that the bride beckons the King to come "like a gazelle or a young stag...on the *mountains of spices*." Messiah Jesus ascended to heaven from the *Mount* of Olives, and we read in the Book of Acts that He "will come in just the same way as you have watched Him go into heaven" (Acts 1:11). The implication is that just as He ascended from the Mount of Olives (Acts 1:12), so will He return.

The Old Testament also foretells of the Messiah returning on the Mount of Olives. Zechariah prophesied:

> In that day His feet will stand on the Mount of Olives, which is in front of Jerusalem on the east; and the Mount of Olives will be split....Then the Lord, my God, will come, and all the holy ones with Him!
>
> —ZECHARIAH 14:4–5

Paralleling God's Word in Zechariah and the Book of Acts, the Song ends with the bride calling for Yeshua to come down from heaven "on the mountains of spices" clothed with the power of God. What an incredible finale, bringing our journey into divine love to its culmination!

As I've said, I see the Song of Songs as a prophetic lens through which to view our relationship with God. The ancient rabbis have interpreted the Song in much the same way, as a description of God's love for Israel, even claiming that it is the holy of holies of the Bible. Rabbi Akiva, one of Israel's most famous and beloved sages, born in AD 50 (close to the time of Yeshua's earthly ministry), said, "All of the writings in the Bible are holy and the Song of Songs is the holiest of holies."[1]

As we close, let's review. The Song begins with the bride encountering the Bridegroom. She is then taken on a long journey through which she is eventually matured and transformed into the image of a servant. And finally at the end of the Song, she is pictured eagerly waiting for her lover and King to return on the mountains of spices, even as we are awaiting our Messiah's return to the top of the Mount of Olives.

Wow! That's all I can say.

The Song so speaks to me, and I hope it greatly blesses you as well!

> He who testifies to these things says, "Yes, I am coming quickly."
>
> —REVELATION 22:20

NOTES

Chapter 11

1. Blue Letter Bible, s.v. "šaḏ," accessed December 7, 2023, https://www.blueletterbible.org/lexicon/h7699/kjv/wlc/0-1/.

Chapter 17

1. Yakov Z. Meyer, "Parashat Song of Songs A 'Handle' for the Torah," Haaretz, April 17, 2014, https://www.haaretz.com/jewish/portion-of-the-week/2014-04-17/ty-article/.premium/parashat-song-of-songs-a-handle-for-the-torah/0000017f-e11a-d9aa-afff-f95a0eb80000.

DISCOVERING THE JEWISH JESUS

CONNECT
WITH RABBI SCHNEIDER

www.DiscoveringTheJewishJesus.com

▶️ /Discovering the Jewish Jesus with Rabbi Schneider

f facebook.com/rabbischneider

🐦 @RabbiSchneider

Roku Roku—Discovering the Jewish Jesus

📺tv Apple TV—Discovering the Jewish Jesus

available at **amazon** appstore Amazon App—Discovering the Jewish Jesus

🎙️ Podcast—Discovering the Jewish Jesus

Search for Rabbi Schneider and Discovering the Jewish Jesus on your favorite platform.

For a complete list of Rabbi Schneider's television and radio broadcasts, visit www.DiscoveringTheJewishJesus.com.